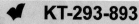

KT-293-893

AS Law

UNIT 2

AQA

Module 2: Dispute Solving

Ian Yule

Philip Allan Updates
Market Place
Deddington
Oxfordshire
OX15 0SE

Tel: 01869 338652
Fax: 01869 337590
e-mail: sales@philipallan.co.uk
www.philipallan.co.uk

© Philip Allan Updates 2003

ISBN 0 86003 932 3

This guide has been written specifically to support students preparing for the
AQA AS Law Unit 2 examination. The content has been neither approved nor
endorsed by AQA and remains the sole responsibility of the author.

Printed by Information Press, Eynsham, Oxford

Contents

Introduction

■ ■ ■

Content Guidance

■ ■ ■

Questions and Answers

Introduction

About this guide

The AQA specification for the AS and A2 Law examinations is divided into six modules. AS Unit 2 deals with **dispute solving**. The topics within this part of the specification are designed to provide a sound introduction to the way the English legal system works; they cover the different types of courts and the alternatives to courts, lawyers, judges, the particular importance of lay people, and the ways in which access to justice is ensured.

There are three sections to this guide:
- **Introduction** — this provides advice on how this guide should be used, an explanation of the skills required to complete the unit successfully and guidance on revision techniques.
- **Content Guidance** — this sets out the specification content for Unit 2, breaking it down into manageable sections for study and learning. It also contains references to cases which you will need to study for a sound understanding of each topic.
- **Questions and Answers** — this section provides nine sample AS questions. All questions are followed by a A-grade answer; some of them are also followed by a C-grade answer. An examiner's comments show how marks are awarded or why they are withheld.

How to use this guide

While the Content Guidance covers all the elements of the Unit 2 specification, it is not intended to be a comprehensive and detailed set of notes for the unit — the material needs to be supplemented by further reading from textbooks and case studies.

At the end of each section, make a summary of the factual material under the appropriate headings, incorporating additional material from your wider reading and research, and then test yourself by using the sample question(s) on that particular topic. By practising questions and assessing your answers against the examiner's comments you will learn how to use your knowledge and understanding effectively to improve your exam grade.

Learning strategies

It is essential to build up a good set of notes for successful AS study. Your notes need to be laid out clearly under headings, as in the Content Guidance section. They should contain accurate definitions, using the correct legal terminology, detailed explanation and relevant case and statutory references. It is recommended that you compile summaries of the most important cases.

Revision planning

At this level of study, it is essential that you understand the need to learn the basic factual information thoroughly as the module is being taught. Do not leave it to the 'revision stage', otherwise you will find that there is simply too much detailed knowledge to absorb — there is a real danger that facts from different sections will become confused (frequently a cause of problems in candidates' examination answers).

The word 'revise' is defined in the *Concise Oxford Dictionary* as to 'read again (work learnt or done) to improve one's knowledge'. Simply skimming over some notes or reading this guide is *not* revision if you have not already learnt the material.

The first stage of successful revision requires organisation of all your work. You should ensure that:
- your class notes are up to date
- you have used the material in this guide effectively
- you have made accurate notes on any wider reading, especially of case studies

The final key stage is to prepare a summary of all the material, organised under the headings and subheadings within the unit specification. The revision period is the time for going over all your notes and reducing them to manageable proportions, which is, in itself, an effective learning exercise. The act of summarising makes it easier to recall the material and should reduce the chance of forgetting parts of it in the examination. The greatest number of marks are lost not through factual mistakes but by simply omitting material or explanation.

Assessment objectives

Assessment objectives (AOs) are common to AS and A2 units and are intended to assess candidates' ability to:
- recall, select, deploy and develop knowledge and understanding of legal principles accurately and by means of examples
- analyse legal material, issues and situations, and evaluate and apply the appropriate legal rules and principles
- present a logical and coherent argument and communicate relevant material in a clear and effective manner, using correct legal terminology

Content
Guidance

The specification for Unit 2 outlined in this section covers the following topics:

Lay people

Juries — qualifications, selection and role of jurors.

Magistrates — selection and appointment, training, role and powers.

Legal professions

Qualifications and training of solicitors, barristers and legal executives, and the work undertaken by each. Role of professional bodies and disciplinary processes.

Judges

Selection and appointment, training, functions in different types of court, dismissal procedures and judicial independence.

The courts system

Trial and appellate jurisdiction of both civil and criminal courts; outline knowledge of civil process; promotion of pre-trial settlement, allocation of cases to appropriate court, relative informality of small claims track; routes of and grounds of appeal; advantages and disadvantages of courts.

Outline knowledge of criminal process; classification of offences — summary, 'either-way' and indictable; bail and remand; mode of trial by magistrates' and crown courts; routes and grounds of appeal.

Alternatives to courts

Functions of tribunals and arbitration; mediation, conciliation and negotiation; comparison of these alternatives with each other and with civil courts in terms of cost, time, formality, representation, accessibility and appropriateness for particular kinds of dispute resolution.

Finance of advice and representation

Private financing, insurance, 'law for free', conditional fee agreements; statutory provision of legal help and representation in both civil and criminal cases; alternative sources of advice, e.g. the Citizens' Advice Bureau (CAB).

Lay people

Juries

The jury system was imported into Britain after the Norman Conquest, though its early functions were quite different from those it fulfils today: the first jurors acted as witnesses, providing information about local matters. Under Henry II, the jurors began to take on an important judicial function, moving from reporting on events they knew about to deliberating on evidence produced by the parties involved in a dispute.

A major milestone in the history of the jury was *Bushell*'s case, where it was finally established that the jury members were the sole judges of fact, had the right to give a verdict according to their conscience and could not be penalised for taking a view of the facts opposed to that of the judge. The importance of this power now is that a jury may acquit a defendant, even when the law demands a guilty verdict.

Juries, although very important in our system of criminal justice, take part in under 1% of all criminal trials — over 96% of criminal trials are conducted in magistrates' courts, approximately 70% of defendants in crown courts plead guilty, and a further proportion of defendants are found not guilty by means of 'directed acquittals', where the trial judge instructs the jury as a matter of law to return a formal verdict of 'not guilty'. In civil cases, juries are only involved in about 200 cases a year, mostly libel cases in the High Court.

Selection of jurors

Before 1972, only those who owned a home over a certain rateable value were eligible for jury service — the Morris Committee in 1965 estimated that 78% of people on the electoral register did not qualify for jury service, and 95% of women were ineligible. The current qualifications for jury service are detailed in the **Juries Act 1974**, which provides that potential jury members must be:
- aged between 18 and 70 years
- on the electoral register
- resident in the UK, Channel Islands or Isle of Man for at least 5 years since the age of 13

The jury summoning officer arranges for potential jurors' names to be picked at random from the electoral register. At court, a final random selection takes place — 12 jurors are selected from 15 to form a jury. However, some people are either excluded or excused under the following categories:
- **Disqualification**
  Those with a criminal conviction who have served a custodial sentence of 3 months within the last 10 years are disqualified for 10 years, as are those who have received a community punishment order. Those who have received a community

content guidance

rehabilitation order are disqualified for 5 years. The length of disqualification depends on the length of sentence imposed. Offenders on bail are also disqualified.

- **Ineligibility**

  Five categories of people are ineligible for jury service:

  (1) the judiciary

  (2) those concerned with the administration of justice, e.g. barristers, solicitors

  (3) police and prison officers

  (4) the clergy

  (5) people with mental health problems and people with a physical disability

- **Excusal as of right**

  People over 65 and any people whose duties are considered more important than jury service (these include MPs, members of the armed forces, doctors, nurses and vets) may choose whether they wish to serve.

- **Excusal at the court's discretion**

  Those with limited understanding of English, students doing public examinations, parents with childcare commitments/problems, or people with prior commitments such as booked holidays etc. may be excused jury service.

Note: at the time of writing, the Criminal Justice Bill 2003 proposes to end all categories of ineligible people, with the exception of the mentally ill, and to remove the right to be automatically excused by reason of more important public duties.

Jury challenging and vetting

In the UK, challenging a juror is a rare event, but there are three main ways in which it can occur:

(1) Prosecution can use 'Stand by for the Crown' without giving a reason, although the Attorney General announced in 1988 that this right would only be used to remove 'a manifestly unsuitable' juror or to remove a juror in a terrorist/security trial where jury vetting had been authorised.

(2) Defence can challenge 'for cause' which, in terms of a Practice Note in 1973 issued by the Lord Chief Justice, may *not* include race, religion, political beliefs or occupation. A successful challenge is therefore only likely to occur where the juror is personally known. In *R* v *Gough* it was held that, where a juror is challenged on the grounds of possible bias, the test is whether there is 'real danger' that he/she is biased. Note that the right of the defence to use peremptory challenges was abolished by the **Criminal Justice Act 1988**.

(3) Both parties may challenge the whole jury panel — 'challenge to the array' — on the ground that the summoning officer is biased or has acted improperly. This happens very rarely.

The function of the jury

The jurors have to weigh up the evidence and decide what are the true facts of the case — the judge directs them as to what is the relevant law, and the jurors then have to apply that law to the facts that they have found and thereby reach a verdict.

In civil cases, if the jury has found the defendant liable, it then decides on the amount of damages to award. In any case involving a jury, there is a partnership between the judge, who acts as 'master of the law', and the jury, which is 'master of the facts'.

Criminal cases

Juries are used in all serious criminal cases, i.e. indictable offences which are tried at crown court. The number of cases decided by juries is about 60,000 per year. The jury has the sole responsibility for determining guilt; since the **Criminal Justice Act 1967**, majority verdicts are possible (a minimum of ten must agree).

During the trial, after the jury has been sworn in, jurors will be present to hear all the evidence led in the case by the prosecution and defence counsels. Notes may be taken and jurors have the opportunity to question witnesses through the judge. At the end of the defence case and after the closing speeches of counsel, the judge will summarise the evidence in the case and direct the jury on relevant legal issues. In complicated cases, the judge will also provide a structured set of questions to assist the jury in its deliberations. The jury retires to a private room, where it chooses a foreperson to present its verdict. If the jury has not returned with a unanimous verdict after a minimum period of 2 hours 10 minutes, the judge may recall it and advise that a majority verdict may be made under the Criminal Justice Act 1967; about 20% of convictions each year are given by such verdicts.

Civil cases

In the past, most civil cases were tried by juries (as they still are in the USA), but trial by jury in the civil system is now almost obsolete. In *Ward* v *James* (1966), Lord Denning argued that juries should only rarely be used because they find it difficult to assess damages accurately and cannot be expected to know what has been awarded in similar cases. Fewer than 1% of civil cases are tried by a jury — these are mostly libel cases, although they can also include fraud, malicious prosecution and false imprisonment (**Supreme Court Act 1981**).

Coroner's courts

In England and Wales the coroner's courts determine cause of death where death is believed not to be from natural causes. A jury is not commonly used, but in cases involving deaths in custody (either in police stations or prisons) a jury must be summoned, comprising an uneven number of jurors — between 7 and 11.

Are juries representative?

The justification for the use of juries in serious criminal cases is that the 12 people are randomly selected and should therefore comprise a representative sample of the population as a whole. This ideal has come closer with the abolition of the property qualification and the use of computers for random selection. It has been argued that random selection might make a jury less likely to be representative: if, for example, many women are excused through childcare, summoning twice as many women as men might be a better way of achieving a representative section of the community. Research carried out by Professor Zander in 1983 found that women were only slightly under-represented and that non-white people constituted 5% of juries, even though they made up 5.9% of the national population. While this last point is encouraging, it has been argued by the Commission for Racial Equality that consideration has to be given to the racial balance in particular cases. The Commission suggests that, where a case has a racial dimension and the defendant reasonably believes that he/she cannot receive a fair trial from an all-white jury, the judge should have the power to order that three of the jurors come from the same ethnic minority as the defendant or the victim. This recommendation was endorsed by the Runciman Royal Commission on Criminal Justice but has never been implemented (so the decision in *R* v *Ford* (1989) that there is no principle that a jury should be racially balanced still holds). The recommendation, although endorsed by Lord Justice Auld in his Criminal Justice Review, has not been accepted by the government.

In recent years, the representative nature of juries has been threatened by the considerable number of professional people evading jury service. Figures show that in some courts more than one third of people who are asked to sit on juries avoid service. The problem is particularly acute with cases which are likely to last for 5 weeks or more, especially complex fraud trials. This is the reason why, as a result of the Criminal Justice Bill 2003, it will be much more difficult for jurors to be excused from jury service.

Advantages of jury trial

Public participation

Juries allow the ordinary citizen to take part in the administration of justice, so that verdicts are seen to be those of society rather than of the judicial system, which satisfies the constitutional tradition of judgment by one's peers. Lord Denning described jury service as giving 'ordinary folk their finest lesson in citizenship'. A survey commissioned by the Bar Council and the Law Society found that:

- over 80% of those questioned were likely to have more confidence in juries than in other players in the justice system
- over 80% thought that juries were likely to reflect their views and values
- 85% trusted juries to reach the right decision
- 85% thought that juries improved the quality of the justice system

These findings have particular importance when one considers the background of magistrates, who continue to be predominantly white and middle class.

'Layman's equity'

Because juries have the ultimate right to find defendants innocent or guilty, it is argued that they act as a check on officialdom and protect against unjust or oppressive prosecution by reflecting a community sense of justice: 'It is the most democratic form of justice in the world, a protection against the use of overbearing and arbitrary power by governments' (Michael Mansfield QC). By 'bending the law', juries, unlike judges and magistrates, have the power to acquit a defendant where the law demands a guilty verdict. There are several well-known cases of juries using this right to find according to their consciences, often in cases dealing with issues of political and moral controversy, e.g. R v Ponting, R v Kronlid and R v Owen. The importance of this aspect of the jury's involvement in criminal justice is difficult to assess. In high-profile cases such as Ponting, the jury can be a valuable statement of public feeling to those in authority, but it cannot always be relied upon. Compare the two cases of R v Tisdall and R v Ponting. In Tisdall, the defendant had exposed government wrongdoing by leaking information and, although it was admitted that the leak had been no threat to national security, she was, nevertheless, convicted, unlike Ponting, who had done the same thing.

Better 'decision making'

On the key issue of guilt/innocence it can be argued that even criminal cases which may involve complex issues of law come down to a decision about essential facts, e.g. identification, witness credibility or dishonesty (in a theft case). Such matters are more likely to be decided correctly as a result of discussion between unbiased and legally unqualified people than by a single judge, who can hardly discuss them on his own. Individual jurors form different impressions about the truthfulness of various witnesses and the legal arguments submitted by opposing counsel. It is also suggested that, because most jurors sit only once in criminal trials, they are not 'case-hardened' and take their responsibility seriously.

Recent research by psychologists has indicated that discussions are better organised within groups of seven. As a consequence, it has been suggested that the jury size should be reduced to no more than ten or that a 'facilitator' should be appointed to guide jury deliberation.

Disadvantages or weaknesses of juries

Lack of competence

Sir Frederick Lawton once stated that '[jurors'] level of understanding of cases, and perhaps their level of intelligence, are not always up to the task they have to perform'. Lord Denning, too, argued that the selection of jurors is too wide, resulting in juries that are not competent to perform their tasks. He went on to suggest that jurors should be selected in much the same way as magistrates are, through interviews and references. This throws up several obvious problems: it would be a complicated and expensive process; a jury that is intelligent and educated can still be biased; the essential argument in favour of juries — that they are randomly selected — would be destroyed.

Particular concern has been expressed about the average jury's understanding of complex fraud cases. The Roskill Committee concluded that trial by random jury was not a satisfactory way of achieving justice in such cases, since many jurors were 'out of their depth'. Ingman points out that through 'inexperience and ignorance' jurors may rely too heavily on what they are told by lawyers at the expense of the real issues. However, the Roskill Committee could not find accurate evidence of a higher proportion of acquittals in complex fraud cases than in any other kind of case; Smith and Bailey in their research found that juries are capable of coming to reasoned and fair verdicts even in complex cases; and police evidence before the Runciman Royal Commission stated that in serious fraud trials the jury actually convicts a slightly higher percentage of cases. Nevertheless, in the Criminal Justice Bill 2003, the government intends to give judges the power to order trial by judge alone for serious and complex fraud trials.

Jury nobbling

Despite the introduction of majority verdicts in the **Criminal Justice Act 1967**, it is believed that jury nobbling remains a major weakness. In 1982, several Old Bailey trials had to be stopped due to attempted nobbling. In 1984, jurors in the *Brinks Mat* trial had to have police protection to and from the court, and their telephone calls were intercepted. A new criminal offence was introduced in the **Criminal Procedure and Investigation Act 1996** to try to give additional protection to juries. It created the offence of intimidating or threatening to harm jurors, and, more radically, s.54 of that Act provided that, where a person has been acquitted and someone is later convicted of interfering with or intimidating jurors or witnesses in the case, the High Court can quash the acquittal and the person can be retried.

Bias

Ingman suggests that jurors may be biased for or against certain groups, e.g. the police. However, in a group of 12 jurors, it is likely that individual bias will be cancelled out by the others. The most conspicuous instance of jury bias has appeared in libel cases where juries prejudiced against tabloid newspapers have awarded huge damages against them, e.g. *Sutcliffe* v *Pressdram*.

Cost

One argument put forward against juries is that crown court jury trials are much more expensive than magistrates' court trials. However, by far the greatest cost elements in the crown court are the costs of lawyers, judges and other court personnel. As most criminal trials last no more than a day, the maximum jury cost is only £500.

Difficulties with appeals

When judges sit alone, their judgment consists of a detailed and explicit finding of fact. When there is a jury, the verdict is returned unexplained: under s.8 of the **Contempt of Court Act 1981**, jury deliberations are secret.

Magistrates

About 30,000 lay magistrates try over a million cases a year — over 96% of all criminal cases — while some 100 district judges (magistrates' courts) with a 7-year general advocacy qualification (formerly called stipendiaries) are appointed by the Queen on the recommendation of the Lord Chancellor.

Selection and appointment

Under the **Justices of the Peace Act 1997**, lay magistrates are appointed by the Lord Chancellor on the advice of county local advisory committees. Members of these committees, mostly drawn from the magistracy, are appointed by the Lord Chancellor; they are supposed to have good local knowledge and to represent a balance of political opinion. Candidates are sometimes put forward to the committee by local political parties, voluntary groups, trade unions and other organisations, though it is becoming more common for individuals to apply in response to advertisements.

The only qualifications for appointment to the magistracy are that the applicants must be under 65 and live within 15 miles of the area for which they are to act. Although there is no statutory minimum age for appointment, in practice no one under the age of 27 is appointed. Applicants must be able to devote, on average, half a day a week to the task, for which only expenses and a small loss of earnings allowance are given. Certain people are excluded: police officers, traffic wardens, probation officers and members of their immediate families; members of the armed forces; those with certain criminal convictions; and undischarged bankrupts.

In 1998, the Lord Chancellor revised the procedures for appointing lay magistrates, aiming to make the criteria open and clear. A job description was introduced, which states that the six key qualities defining the personal suitability of candidates are:
- good character
- understanding and communication
- social awareness
- maturity and sound temperament
- sound judgment
- commitment and reliability

The advisory committee arranges interviews for shortlisted candidates after their references have been checked. There are two interviews: the first examines the candidate's character; the second, comprising sentencing and trial exercises, assesses the candidate's judgment. After the interviews, potential appointees are reviewed by the local advisory subcommittee to ensure that a 'balanced bench' can be achieved in terms of age, gender, ethnic background and occupation. The committee submits its recommendations to the Lord Chancellor, who usually accepts them and makes the appointment. The final stage is the 'swearing-in' of new magistrates by a senior circuit judge. They can be removed by the Lord Chancellor at any time, but this is only done in cases where an individual is deemed to have misbehaved or acted in a way which is inconsistent with the office. Magistrates usually have to retire at 70.

Training

Training is organised by the Judicial Studies Board and is carried out by a team of legal advisers, supported by appropriate professionals such as psychiatrists, probation officers, lawyers and judges. On appointment, all magistrates receive an intensive induction course to familiarise them with court procedures and the theory and practice of sentencing. Since 1998, the amount of training has intensified with the appointment of experienced magistrates as mentors, who support the training and development. New magistrates are assessed within 2 years of their appointment to ensure they have acquired the necessary competencies.

Magistrates who sit in youth courts or on family court panels receive additional training, as do magistrates who wish to become court chairmen. As new laws dealing with sentencing are passed, more resources will be needed for magistrate training, both in terms of time and financial expenditure.

Criminal jurisdiction

Lay magistrates generally sit in groups of three and in criminal cases have four main functions:

(1) Hearing applications for bail — **Bail Act 1976** — and legal aid.

(2) Trial of all summary offences and the majority of 'either-way' offences. They are advised on matters of law by legal advisers, but they alone decide the facts, interpret the law and, where they convict, decide the sentence and any costs and compensation.

(3) Dealing with appeals — in ordinary appeals against conviction from the magistrates' courts to the crown court, (usually two) magistrates sit with a circuit judge.

(4) Dealing with requests for arrest and search warrants from the police.

Youth court

The procedure in the youth court is similar to but less formal than the proceedings of adult courts. They are held in the presence of three magistrates and the justice's clerk. The magistrates concerned in youth courts must have received additional training and there must be a mixed-gender bench. A parent or guardian must be present, and the youth may have a legal representative or social worker. Unlike the adult court, the hearing is held in private and the defendant's name is not disclosed to the public unless it is in the public interest. If found guilty, the young person will be bound over, or receive a deferred sentence, community sentence, or, if he/she is over 15, a sentence of detention in a young offenders institution. If the offender is aged 12–14 and is convicted of a sufficiently serious offence and judged to be a persistent offender, a new sentence under the **Criminal Justice and Public Order Act 1994** may be given — a detention and training order (maximum 2 years, of which 12 months will be under supervision). Other sentences include a fine or absolute or conditional discharges, an antisocial behaviour order (ASBO) or an attendance centre order (for 10–20-year-olds). A referral order is relevant only for first-time offenders who have pleaded guilty; it is set at between 3 and 12 months, depending on the seriousness of the offence. The referral is to a local youth offender panel, which draws up a 'contract' of aims targeted at addressing the offending behaviour. A defendant aged between 10 and 17 can be issued with a supervision order, whereby a social worker is to 'advise, assist and befriend'.

Procedure for indictable offences

Section 51 of the **Crime and Disorder Act 1998** states that for indictable-only offences, adults appearing in the magistrates' court should 'be sent forthwith' to the crown court. Submissions of 'no case to answer' are now part of the pre-trial procedure at the crown court. This process removes the former committal powers of magistrates in such cases.

Civil jurisdiction

Licensing court

The licensing court has the responsibility of granting licences for the sale of alcohol and for betting and gaming establishments. Note that under the Licensing Bill 2003 these powers will be conferred on local authorities, although magistrates will then have an appellate jurisdiction.

Family court

Since the implementation in 1991 of the **Children Act 1989**, the magistrates' family proceedings courts have worked in parallel with the county courts. Cases are usually assigned to the county courts on the grounds of legal complexity, conflicting expert opinion or high profile. Family courts deal with care orders, supervision orders and emergency protection orders. They also have jurisdiction over parental responsibility and contact orders. Adoptions come to the family court for the making of final orders.

Civil debt enforcement

Payment of debts such as council tax or utility (water, gas and electricity) bills are enforced by magistrates.

Powers of magistrates

The maximum term of imprisonment that can be imposed by magistrates is 6 months, unless there are two or more charges which can carry a term of imprisonment, in which case a total of 12 months can be imposed. The maximum fine that magistrates can impose is £5,000. The **Courts Bill 2002** proposes to increase the maximum custodial sentence to 12 months for a single offence. In the youth court, magistrates have the power to sentence a young offender to 2 years' youth custody. It should be noted that in no other European jurisdiction do lay judges have so much power.

Justices' clerks and legal advisers

Because the lay magistrates are not legally qualified and possess only an elementary knowledge of criminal law, it is the function of the justices' clerk or the legal adviser to sit in court with the magistrates' bench, to administer the court and to advise the justices on points of administrative and substantive law and on sentencing. Nationally, there are about 250 full-time justices' clerks to run the courts and about 1,300 legal advisers, of whom 25% are sufficiently legally qualified to act as deputies to the justices' clerks. The qualification for a justices' clerk is 5 years' standing as a barrister or solicitor. Note that in *R* v *Eccles Justices* the Queen's Bench divisional court ruled that a magistrate's decision could not stand because the legal adviser had acted outside his powers when he retired with the magistrates for 25 of the 30 minutes of their retirement from the courtroom. The suggestion was that he participated in the decision-making process.

District judges

District judges in magistrates' courts are legally qualified, paid judges, who have been barristers or solicitors for at least 7 years. They are appointed to courts in large cities or within a county. Retirement is at the age of 70, unless the Lord Chancellor permits an extension.

Advantages of the magistracy

Cost
In 1989 the system cost about £200 million per year to run and brought in a total income of almost £270 million in fines. Lay magistrates try the majority of criminal cases. To pay professional judges to deal with such an enormous caseload would be hugely expensive — at least £100 million per year in salaries alone, plus the cost of appointment and training — and it would take a long time to amass the required number of legally qualified candidates. Switching to crown court trials would be even more expensive.

Lay involvement
The advantage of lay involvement is substantially that cited in support of the jury (layman's equity, see pp. 12–13), but it is questionable because of the restricted social background of magistrates. However, their living within a reasonable distance of the court may provide them with a better-informed picture of local life than judges might have. Note that in recent years many more magistrates from ethnic minorities have been appointed — almost 7% of the national figure.

Weight of numbers
The simple fact that magistrates must usually sit in threes may make a balanced view more likely — in a real sense they sit as a 'mini-jury'.

Disadvantages of the magistracy

Inconsistency
There is considerable inconsistency in the decision making of different benches, particularly noticeable in the awards of legal aid and the type of sentences ordered. Research has confirmed that some benches are over ten times more likely to impose a custodial sentence than neighbouring benches for similar offences.

Bias towards the police
Police officers are frequent witnesses and become well known to magistrates. It has been argued that this results in an almost automatic tendency to believe police

evidence. In *R* v *Bingham JJ ex parte Jowitt*, a speeding case where the only evidence was that of the motorist and a policeman, the chairman of the bench said that where there was direct conflict between the defendant and the police 'my principle...has always been to believe the evidence of the police officer'. The conviction was quashed because of this remark, which was severely criticised.

'Cheap/amateur' justice argument

Because the chances of acquittal are substantially higher in the crown court than in magistrates' courts, the suspicion is created that the crown court is a fairer forum in which to decide cases or even that magistrates are not as fair as they might be. It should be noted, however, that over 90% of defendants plead guilty in magistrates' courts, and the nature of most cases depends more on factual issues, such as drink-driving, than complex legal problems.

Increasing complexity of the law

Many crimes are being downgraded to summary offences, and new offences are being created. Sentencing has become much more complex in recent years, e.g. curfew orders and antisocial behaviour orders (ASBOs).

Legal professions

In England and Wales, there are two distinct legal professions — barristers and solicitors — and two 'subsidiary' professions — licensed conveyancers and legal executives. What are the qualifications required to become a solicitor, barrister or legal executive?

Solicitors

Qualifications

Usually, solicitors have a university degree but not necessarily a law degree. Any other degree or a non-qualifying law degree has to be followed by the Graduate Diploma in Law (GDL) — a 1-year full-time course. After the law degree or GDL, intending solicitors take the Legal Practice Course (LPC), and then undertake a 2-year training contract with a firm of solicitors, during which they have to complete a 20-day professional skills course. With these qualifications, individuals are entered onto the rolls of the Law Society and are entitled to practise as solicitors. After qualification, solicitors have to continue their professional development by attending various professional courses. While the majority of solicitors who qualify each year are graduates, it is possible to qualify as a fellow of the Institute of Legal Executives (ILEX) and then pass the LPC: about 17% of solicitors qualify this way.

Work

Most of the work of a solicitor involves giving advice to clients and carrying out administrative tasks, including conveyancing (dealing with the legal requirements of buying and selling property) or probate (drafting wills and acting as executors for the estates of deceased persons). Other routine work includes drawing up various kinds of contracts, setting up companies and advising clients on family law problems.

Solicitors can act as advocates and represent clients in both magistrates' and county courts, in which they have 'rights of audience'. The opportunity to obtain rights of audience for the higher courts (crown and High Court, and appellate courts) was first made possible by the **Courts and Legal Services Act 1990**, and was extended in the **Access to Justice Act 1999**. For rights of audience, solicitors have to qualify as solicitor-advocates. There are currently over 1,000 solicitor-advocates (out of a total number of 86,000 solicitors).

Solicitors as a group actually do more advocacy work than barristers since 97% of all criminal cases are tried in magistrates' courts, where both the prosecuting and the defending lawyer are solicitors.

Even where a barrister has been instructed to represent the client in a court case, the solicitor still has an important role in the overall litigation process, handling various procedural aspects of the case such as evidence-gathering and discovery of documents.

Solicitors usually work in partnerships. There has been a trend in recent years for firms of solicitors to merge into larger partnerships, which in turn has led to increasing specialisation.

Barristers

Qualifications

Barristers must be graduates, although their degree need not be in law (if it is not, they must take the GDL).

In order to continue their professional training, intending barristers must become a member of one of the four Inns of Court. These are independent of one another and all have libraries, award scholarships and organise lectures and moots (mock trials). Before being 'called to the Bar' by their Inn, the student must be accepted for and complete the Bar Vocational Course (BVC), which comprises the practical skills of advocacy and drafting pleadings and negotiation; the student must also have 'dined in' on 12 occasions (this rule now includes attending residential courses).

Having been called to the Bar on passing the BVC, the student must obtain a 1-year pupillage at a set of chambers with an experienced barrister, who acts as a 'pupil master'. After the first 6 months of pupillage, barristers can appear in court in minor cases by themselves. A programme of continuing education is organised by the Bar Council during this period. To practise as an independent barrister (as a member of the Bar), the barrister finally has to secure a tenancy in a set of chambers. Both processes (obtaining a pupillage and securing a tenancy) are very difficult as demand outstrips supply. There are currently no more than 650 pupillages and 300–350 tenancies available.

Work

Barristers belong to a 'referral profession': this means that members of the public cannot go to them directly but first have to consult a solicitor, who will then instruct a barrister if it is considered necessary. This process is similar to that of seeing a general practitioner first with a medical problem, and then being referred by the GP to a hospital consultant if the problem is serious. Barristers may, however, be engaged directly by certain professionals, e.g. accountants, and, since 1996, by members of the public whose cases have been handled by Citizens' Advice Bureau (CAB) staff.

Barristers are obliged under the 'cab-rank' rule to accept any case referred to them, provided it lies within their legal expertise, the appropriate fee has been agreed and they are free at the time to accept the brief. This means that barristers cannot refuse to accept instructions in a case on the grounds of their own beliefs, the nature of the case or the character of the person on whose behalf they are instructed.

Most of the work of barristers involves advocacy in any court as they have full rights of audience in all English courts. The other main activity of barristers is that of providing counsel's opinions to solicitors on behalf of clients who require a specialised second opinion.

Barristers are self-employed and work from a set of chambers with other barristers, who share administrative and accommodation expenses. A clerk is employed, whose work involves booking cases and negotiating fees.

After 10 years in practice, barristers may apply to the Lord Chancellor to become Queen's Counsel or QC, called 'taking silk', as they wear a court gown made of silk. About 10% of barristers are QCs. Becoming a QC is a required step for most barristers if they aspire to be circuit or High Court judges.

Legal executives

Most firms of solicitors employ legal executives, who do much of the basic work of solicitors — especially conveyancing and probate. Their qualifications are laid down by ILEX. Trainee legal executives have to pass Parts I and II of ILEX and then work for 5 years in a solicitor's firm (or other legal organisation, e.g. the Crown Prosecution Service (CPS)) in order to become a Fellow of ILEX.

Role of professional bodies

The Law Society

The Law Society has a number of functions. It regulates admission, qualifications and training, including continuing professional development, for all solicitors and issues practising certificates. It promotes the interests of solicitors and deals with disciplinary matters and complaints.

Discipline

In 1996, the Solicitors' Complaints Bureau (SCB), which had been criticised, was replaced by the Office for the Supervision of Solicitors (OSS), which was designed to be more efficient and client-friendly. The OSS gave lay members a greater role in order to increase the office's independence from the profession.

Clients' minor complaints are sent to the firms concerned to be resolved, since part of the OSS's role has been to encourage law firms to develop better client care practices (in 1996, it found that one firm in four had no in-house complaints procedure).

However, the OSS has been as severely criticised as the SCB, its ill-fated predecessor, by the legal services ombudsman and the Consumers' Association. In 2001, its chief executive was forced to resign after he wrote to a complainant to advise her that the complaint could not be investigated for about a year. The Lord Chancellor formally warned the Law Society that unless it 'put its house in order' it would lose its right to self-regulation. In 2002, the OSS was considerably strengthened in terms of personnel and operating budgets and appears to be handling complaints much more effectively.

In 2002, the OSS received almost 15,000 complaints (an increase of 37%) from clients dissatisfied with their treatment by solicitors. Serious complaints are referred either straight to the solicitors' disciplinary tribunal or through the OSS to the tribunal.

The disciplinary tribunal has the power to suspend, fine, strike off, or impose conditions on solicitors. In recent years, more solicitors are being struck off than ever before. Appeals from this tribunal go to the High Court.

The Bar Council

The Bar Council has overall control of practising barristers, and its members come from all sections of the Bar. Its functions include making general policy decisions, determining the consolidated regulations for the Inns of Court, dealing with disciplinary matters and making provisions for the education and training of barristers.

Discipline

In 1997 the Bar Council appointed its first Complaints Commissioner, who can require barristers to reduce, refund or waive fees and can order compensation of up to £2,000. More serious complaints will be referred to the Professional Conduct and Complaints Committee, which can decide to dismiss the complaint or to find the barrister guilty of misconduct. It has the power to fine barristers up to £5,000, to suspend or to disbar them. In 2000, in a major change of the law, the case of *Hall* v *Simons* overturned the earlier case of *Rondel* v *Worsley*, thus removing barristers' immunity from being sued for professional negligence in respect of work in court.

Legal services ombudsman

Complainants who are dissatisfied with the way their grievances are handled by either profession can ask the ombudsman to investigate. The number of cases being accepted by the ombudsman is, in 2003, at an all-time high. Between January 1998 and March 1999, the ombudsman conducted 1,658 investigations concerning both solicitors and barristers.

Social background of lawyers

The legal profession as a whole has traditionally come from a very narrow social background in terms of class, race and sex. This is, of course, a problem in several other areas of professional life in the UK. In the law, as elsewhere, the main disadvantage of these barriers is that they prevent the profession from attracting the best minds that the country has to offer.

Lawyers are mainly middle class — evidence to the Royal Commission on Legal Services (RCLS) stated that the parental occupation of 60.9% of its solicitor students and 67.3% of its bar students was either professional or managerial.

A major contributory factor to this situation has been the lack of funding for legal training, which has made it very difficult for students without well-off parents to qualify, especially as barristers. In recent years, the difficulties have worsened as short-ages of funds have meant that local education authorities (LEAs) have become more reluctant to award discretionary grants even to cover fees, let alone living expenses. A survey by the Law Society in 1992 found that of the 102 LEAs which replied, only six would consider giving discretionary grants to students on the GDL course and 57 to students on the LPC. Even these did not undertake to give grants to all applicants, and grants, when given, rarely covered more than a percentage of tuition fees. Maintenance grants were only given in exceptional circumstances and would only cover a percentage of living expenses.

Women remain under-represented in both legal professions, although in terms of entry women now make up 62% of Law Society entrants, 59% of trainee solicitors and about 50% of new barristers. However, there are significant problems when one considers the relatively few women who are QCs or partners in solicitors' firms. In 1996, a survey by the Law Society found that differences in pay ranged from an average of £3,000 between male and female assistant solicitors, to as much as £15,000 between men and women at partner level. At the Bar, only 5 out of the 67 new QCs in 1997 were women. Only 3 judges (out of 36) in the Court of Appeal and 6 (out of 107) High Court judges are women.

These factors create further problems for the legal profession in that the narrow social background of most lawyers means that the professions are seen as unapproachable and elitist, which can deter some people from using lawyers and thereby defending their legal rights. The judiciary is drawn from the legal professions and this must therefore tend to produce judges with a similarly narrow background.

Recent changes in the legal professions

Solicitors

(1) Removal of monopoly conveyancing rights in the **Administration of Justice Act 1985** and the creation of licensed conveyancers.

(2) By the **Courts and Legal Services Act 1990** higher court rights of audience are granted to solicitor-advocates. There are now over 1,000 solicitor-advocates. Note Linklater's announcement in 2001 that all litigation lawyers in firm are to qualify as solicitor-advocates, and that virtually all litigation will be 'in-house'. Higher judicial appointments opened up to solicitors. Multidisciplinary partnerships have become a possibility, subject to regulations of Law Society.

(3) Increasing specialisation of profession; importance of continuing professional development.

(4) Merger of smaller firms, and movement to international partnerships. Clifford Chance has become the world's largest firm of solicitors.

(5) Increasing number of women applicants — 52% of new solicitors in 1998.

(6) Nowadays, the majority of top law graduates from Oxbridge enter the solicitors' profession, not the Bar.

(7) Much improved complaints process. Establishment of OSS.

(8) **Access to Justice Act 1999** — should lead to full rights of audience for solicitors, once the Law Society provides specialist advocacy training.

Barristers

(1) Direct professional access — certain professions, e.g. accountants, can consult barristers directly without being referred by solicitors.

(2) Direct client access to barristers working in law centres.

(3) Rules relaxed on the location of sets of chambers in London — previously barristers could only work in Inns of Court.

(4) Increasing number of women entrants to the Bar — 46% in 1998.

(5) Greater number of women judges.

(6) Greater specialisation and Continuing Professional Development (CPD).

(7) More female QCs: 10 were appointed in 2001, instead of the 'usual' 4, and 13 in 2002.

(8) First woman chairman of the Bar Council, Heather Hallett (now a High Court judge).

(9) First woman appointed Head of Division, Dame Elizabeth Butler-Sloss, President of Family Division.

(10) Creation of Complaints Commissioner to deal with complaints against barristers.

(11) *Hall* v *Simons* overturned rule in *Rondel* v *Worsley* — barristers and solicitors can now be sued for negligence in court work.

(12) Rules against employed barristers having rights of audience are being relaxed. Crown Prosecution Service barristers and solicitor-advocates are now allowed to prosecute in crown court. In July 2001, the Director of Public Prosecutions (DPP) prosecuted in a crown court trial for the first time. In September 2001, the Bar Council advised the Lord Chancellor that it had dropped its objection to employed barristers having rights of audience.

(13) Barristers may now advertise — discreetly.

(14) In 2001, the Bar Council approved salaries for pupil barristers.

(15) In 2002, following criticism by the Office of Fair Trading (OFT) in 2001, the Bar Council passed a resolution agreeing in principle to direct public access to barristers for legal advice. The initial view is that this could lead to suspected offenders being able to consult barristers directly in police stations.

Judges

Our judiciary still consists almost exclusively of middle-aged to elderly men who worked as barristers for 20 years or more prior to their appointment. No one used to be able to become a High Court judge unless he or she had been a barrister of at least 10 years' standing. This rule was changed by the **Courts and Legal Services Act 1990**, whereby appointments to the High Court could be made from those (including solicitor-advocates) who had a 10-year High Court qualification or from circuit judges in post for at least 2 years. The first High Court appointment of a solicitor — Michael Sachs, who had been a circuit judge — was made in 1994.

All Lords Justices of Appeal and Law Lords, our most senior judges, were formerly barristers. Barristers previously had the exclusive right to senior judicial posts, and the predominance of barristers among those appointed to the circuit bench has certain advantages, which are to the public interest in that they are expert in both the law and court procedures. However, there have been significant changes to the qualifications and procedures for judicial appointment over recent years. The **Courts and Legal Services Act 1990** laid down the current statutory criteria for the appointment of each level of judge.

Statutory criteria

District judge	7 years as solicitor or barrister
Recorder (part-time judge)	10 years' rights of audience in crown or county courts

Circuit judge	10 years' rights of audience in crown or county courts
High Court judge	10 years' rights of audience in High Court
Lord Justice of Appeal	10 years' rights of audience in High Court
Lord of Appeal-in-Ordinary	15 years' rights of audience in High Court and the holding of high judicial office for at least 2 years

Appointment procedures

For district judges, recorders and circuit judges, the procedure is the same. Advertisements are placed by the Lord Chancellor's Department (LCD) in newspapers and professional journals, and on the LCD's website. Suitably qualified candidates apply by filling in an application form and providing a number of personal referees. After taking up these references and the usual 'secret soundings', the LCD shortlists the candidates, who are interviewed by a panel comprising a circuit judge, an official from the Judicial Appointments Department in the Lord Chancellor's Department and a lay person. Successful candidates are recommended to the Lord Chancellor, who formally makes the appointment.

Candidates for the position of High Court judge apply in response to an advertisement, as above, but the Lord Chancellor retains the right to invite 'suitably qualified candidates' to apply. The selection process requires all serving High Court judges to provide an opinion on each candidate. 'Secret soundings' are taken by officials in the Lord Chancellor's Department, and a review of shortlisted candidates is undertaken by the Lord Chancellor together with all Heads of Divisions. The Lord Chancellor then makes the appointment, and the new judge is assigned to one of the three Divisions of the High Court.

For the most senior judicial positions — Lord Justice of Appeal and Law Lord — the Lord Chancellor recommends candidates to the prime minister, who advises the Queen. Such judges will have been High Court judges or (for appointment as Law Lords) Court of Appeal judges, although for the House of Lords, which is the UK supreme court, two Scottish judges are usually selected, drawn from the Inner House of the Court of Session (the Scottish Civil Court of Appeal). One senior judge is chosen from Northern Ireland, often the former Lord Chief Justice of the province.

Note

At the time of writing (June 2003), in the process of a cabinet reshuffle, the prime minister indicated the end of the position of Lord Chancellor as Speaker of the House of Lords and as Head of the Judiciary. To replace the Lord Chancellor, Tony Blair proposed that Lord Falconer would sit in the Cabinet as 'Secretary of State for Constitutional Affairs' and that the appointment of new judges would become the responsibility of an independent Judicial Appointments Commission. The final change likely to take place is the creation of a new Supreme Court whose members will no longer sit as Life Peers and will therefore not be able to take part in House of Lords debates.

Training

As all judges were formerly either barristers or solicitors, they are already highly skilled in legal knowledge and court procedure. This professional background has in the past led judges to believe that further training is unnecessary. In this country, judges still receive less training to be judges than is the case in other countries, where there are 'career judges', law graduates who decide to train as judges without first qualifying as lawyers. This problem is compounded by the fact that many judges are appointed to try cases where they have no relevant expertise. It is quite common for recorders, whose principal duty is to try 'either-way' offences in crown courts, to be selected from barristers or solicitors who have little criminal court experience. High Court judges are also not infrequently assigned to a Division in which they have little direct experience.

Trainee recorders receive a $3\frac{1}{2}$-day training course, during which they are given specific training in sentencing law and procedures at crown court. They also visit a prison as part of their training. Before presiding over a crown court trial, they sit alongside an experienced circuit judge.

In recent years the Judicial Studies Board, which oversees all judicial training, has received large increases in its operating budget and has arranged more courses for judges and magistrates, including courses in ethnic awareness, human rights and computer use. The civil procedure rules — reforms to the civil justice system — have prompted further judicial training.

Functions

To understand the different functions of judges, it is necessary to distinguish between the different levels in the hierarchy of judges and the courts over which they preside.

Generally, in civil courts, judges preside over the court, decide legal issues concerning admissibility of evidence and give a reasoned decision in favour of one of the parties. If the defendant is held liable, the judge decides the award of damages. In criminal cases tried in crown courts, the judge ensures that order is maintained, summarises evidence to the jury and directs them on relevant legal rules. If the defendant is convicted, the judge decides the sentence to be imposed. In appeal cases, judges have an important 'law-making' role through the operation of the doctrine of precedent and statutory interpretation.

- **District judges** work in both county courts, where they preside over small claims cases and have administrative responsibilities, and magistrates' courts.
- **Recorders** (part-time) work in both crown courts and county courts.
- **Circuit judges**, like recorders, sit in both crown and county courts.
- **High Court judges**, on appointment, are assigned to a specific Division of the High Court. Queen's Bench judges go on circuit to crown courts, where they try all Class 1 offences (such as murder) and most Class 2 offences (all other serious

offences for which a life sentence could be imposed). They also sit in the Court of Appeal (Criminal Division) together with a Lord Justice of Appeal.

- **Lords Justices of Appeal** sit in the Court of Appeal, either in the Civil or Criminal Division, usually in a panel of three.
- **Law Lords** sit in the House of Lords (Appellate Committee), where they hear final appeals, which must involve a point of law of 'general public importance'. Only about 70 cases are heard each year, the majority being tax cases. These judges also sit in the Judicial Committee of the Privy Council to hear cases from the few Commonwealth countries which allow such appeals to the UK, and from Scotland under the **Scotland (Devolution) Act 1998**.
- **Senior judges** are asked by government ministers to preside over judicial or public enquiries, e.g. the Dunblane Enquiry (Lord Cullen), the Hillsborough football disaster (Mr Justice Taylor), and the 'Arms to Iraq' Enquiry (Lord Scott).

Judicial independence

In our legal system great importance is attached to the idea that judges should be independent from any pressure from the government, particularly, or from any political or other groups. This is to guarantee that they are free to decide cases impartially (see Article 6 in the European Convention of Human Rights, which was incorporated into UK law by the **Human Rights Act 1998**).

Judicial independence is essential to the theory of the 'rule of law'. Dicey analysed this important concept in the nineteenth century and stated that 'no person is punishable except for a distinct breach of the law established in the courts' and not only is no man 'above the law, but that every man, whatever be his rank, is subject to the ordinary law of the realm'.

This theory of judicial independence owes its origin to the classical theory of 'the separation of powers' first discussed by Montesquieu, who argued that the only way to safeguard individual liberties is to ensure that the power of the state is divided between three separate and independent arms: the legislature, the executive and the judiciary. The idea is that each arm should operate independently, so that each one is checked and balanced by the other two. At the time of writing (June 2003), this issue is the subject of controversy involving both the Home Secretary and Lord Chancellor.

The separation of powers works in the following ways:
- **Tenure of office**. In England all judges of the Supreme Court (excluding the Lord Chancellor) hold office 'during good behaviour', subject to removal only by the monarch by means of an address presented by both Houses of Parliament (**Act of Settlement 1701**). This has never happened to an English judge. The Lord Chancellor has laid down new procedures to investigate serious allegations made about circuit judges and other inferior judges. He retains the power of dismissal but may only exercise it following an investigation into any such allegations by a senior judge appointed by the Lord Chief Justice (LCJ) and further discussion with, and agreement of, the LCJ and other senior judges.

- **Judicial immunity from suit**. No judge may be sued in respect for anything done while acting in his/her judicial capacity.
- **Immunity from parliamentary criticism**. No criticism of an individual judge may be made in either House except by way of a substantive motion. Political neutrality is also preserved in that judicial salaries are charged upon the consolidated fund, which removes the opportunity for an annual debate.

Note: full-time judges are excluded from membership of the House of Commons. However, in the House of Lords, all Law Lords and the LCJ are able to speak during debates on particular bills and to vote. In recent years, a number of serving Law Lords became involved in politically contentious debates concerning the administration of justice, penal policy and civil liberties, e.g. the present LCJ, Lord Woolf, opposed the provision in the Criminal Justice Bill 1997 for mandatory sentences. Such examples point up the obvious difficulty that the judges who were actively involved in the passage of legislation in the House of Lords might in the future be the judges who have to decide these same issues in their judicial capacity.

The value of judicial independence is highlighted by the huge increase in judicial review cases, in which judges are required to examine the legality or procedural correctness of government decisions. There have been many instances of government ministers' decisions being overruled by judges.

The independence of the judiciary is particularly necessary when judges have to chair inquiries into major cases and national events, e.g. the Profumo scandals, the Dunblane shootings, the Hillsborough disaster, the Stephen Lawrence murder and the 'arms to Iraq' controversy.

Dismissal

All judges of the Supreme Court — of High Court rank and above — hold office 'during good behaviour'; this means that they may only be dismissed by the monarch following the passing of a substantive critical motion through both Houses of Parliament. This has never happened to an English judge — the only occasion on which this procedure has been invoked was in 1830, when an Irish judge, Sir Jonah Barrington, was dismissed for embezzlement.

It is possible for a judge to be removed on grounds of incapacity — through physical or mental ill-health — but this very much depends on the discretion of the Lord Chancellor. When Lord Chief Justice Lord Widgery became seriously ill towards the end of his judicial career, suffering from a serious degenerative nervous disease which caused him to become 'visibly and distressingly half-senile', he remained in his job.

The only recent example of a High Court judge effectively resigning because of severe criticism is that of Mr Justice Harman, who resigned following serious criticism of him for taking over 18 months to deliver a reserved judgment in the Court of Appeal.

As regards the removal of junior judges (up to the level of circuit judge), the Lord Chancellor has introduced procedures to reflect the **Human Rights Act 1998** — this is summarised in the section on judicial independence above.

Many lawyers and organisations, such as Justice, have argued for the establishment of a Judicial Complaints Commission, which would be an independent body with powers to investigate whether a judge had acted injudiciously. If serious allegations against a judge were upheld, the commission would present these to a tribunal, which could recommend to the Lord Chancellor that a judge should be suspended or dismissed. Such arguments are rejected by judges on the grounds that judicial independence would be undermined.

The courts system

Students need to understand the jurisdiction of the different courts in England and Wales — both civil and criminal — and the process of appeals to the Court of Appeal and the House of Lords.

Civil courts

Civil claims are actions taken by individuals against other individuals and deal principally with areas of contract, tort, land, employment and family law.

County courts

The 300 or so county courts, which are governed by the **County Courts Act 1984**, handle most civil actions. Usually they are presided over by a circuit judge, although recorders and district judges also sit in cases.

The jurisdiction of the county court

The jurisdiction of the county court is very wide. It covers contract and tort actions up to a value of £50,000, has jurisdiction for probate and land law cases, principally repossession orders, and has an equitable jurisdiction which includes bankruptcy and tax cases. If the court is designated a divorce county court, it can hear undefended divorce actions. (Out of 300 county courts, about 170 are divorce courts.) The county court has jurisdiction over a specific locality, within which defendants must live or carry out their business. Note that under the Civil Procedure Rules (CPR), which implemented the Woolf Access to Justice recommendations, all fast-track actions must be taken in the county court. Appeals are heard by a circuit judge (small claims cases), a single High Court judge (fast-track cases) or a Court of Appeal (multi-track cases). In all cases, leave to appeal must be granted.

Small claims arbitration procedure

Within the county court is the small claims arbitration procedure, which currently has a jurisdiction to hear cases up to a value of £5,000 (£1,000 in personal injury cases). A district judge presides over this less formal procedure, where parties are usually unrepresented (as legal aid is not available) and costs are not awarded to the successful party. Most actions heard are for debt recovery and consumer problems. This arbitration has dealt with many cases, which would not have been possible in the county court itself because of the high costs, delay and complexity involved. However, there have been problems over enforcement of court orders: about one third of successful claimants have been unable to recover their award of damages.

The High Court

The High Court is set up in divisions — Queen's Bench (QB), Chancery and Family — of which the QB is the busiest, with over 70 High Court judges assigned to it. There is no financial limit to the jurisdiction of the High Court. While most cases are heard in London, the number of High Court sittings in major cities outside London is increasing.

Queen's Bench divisional court

The Queen's Bench Division traditionally hears contract and tort actions — it alone has jurisdiction to hear defamation (mainly libel) cases. Within the QB Division are the Commercial Court and the Admiralty Court. The QB is the most important of the divisional courts and has three main areas of jurisdiction:

(1) Under the **Magistrates Court Act 1980**, appeal to the QB is by way of 'case stated' on a point of law. The magistrates' court sets out its findings of fact and the prosecution and defence case, together with the legal rules applied, and then asks the QB to determine the question of law in dispute.

(2) The most important and growing area of jurisdiction is that of judicial review, where two judges assess the legality or reasonableness of decisions/actions of public bodies, especially of government ministers.

(3) The QB has general oversight of all inferior courts, tribunals and any body exercising a quasi-judicial function. It regulates this jurisdiction by prerogative orders of certiorari (order directing that a record of proceedings in a lower court be sent up for review), prohibition (order forbidding an inferior court to determine a matter outside its jurisdiction) and mandamus (order commanding an inferior tribunal, public official, corporation etc. to carry out a public duty).

Chancery divisional court

The Chancery Division still mainly exercises an equitable jurisdiction and deals with contested probate matters, trusts, mortgages, bankruptcies, company and partnership cases, and taxation matters.

Family divisional court

This court has jurisdiction over matrimonial matters, including contested divorce actions, wardship, adoption and uncontested probate matters. Note that some of the most difficult legal cases, such as *Bland* v *Airedale NHS Trust* and the '*Siamese Twins*' case in 2000 (Conjoined Twins: Medical Treatment), come before this court.

The Court of Appeal (Civil Division)

Most appeals to this court come from the High Court, but it may also hear appeals from multi-track actions in the county court. Although most appeals involve questions of law, the court will hear appeals over the amount of damages awarded, e.g. in libel cases (see the case of *Sutcliffe* v *Pressdram*). Leave to appeal must be granted either by the lower court or by the Court of Appeal itself. After the hearing, the Appeal Court can reverse or uphold the lower court's decision, vary the award or (rarely) order a retrial.

The House of Lords

Unlike all other courts described above, the House of Lords, when hearing civil cases, sits as a UK court as it takes civil appeals from both Scotland and Northern Ireland. It only hears approximately 70 cases a year, mostly civil, the majority of which concern tax law. The majority of appeals come from the Court of Appeal or the Scottish Court of Session, but it is possible for cases to come directly to the House of Lords from the High Court, using the 'leap-frog' procedure, though this is very rare.

Leave to appeal to the House of Lords must be given either by the lower court, usually the Court of Appeal, or by two Law Lords, where such leave has not been granted. Only cases which raise a point of law of general public importance will be heard here.

Problems with civil courts

Too expensive

Research carried out for Lord Woolf's review found that one side's costs exceeded the amount in dispute in over 40% of cases where the claim was for under £12,500. Where the claim was for between £12,500 and £25,000, average costs were between 40% and 95% of the claim. The bill for one claim of just £2,000 came to £69,295. The survey concluded that the simplest cases often incurred the highest costs in proportion to the value of the claim.

Because of the complexity of the process, lawyers are usually needed. High Court litigation especially is not a game for the inexperienced, so barristers draft the pleadings and advise on the evidence. This is very expensive. The sheer length of civil proceedings also impacts on the costs.

Delays

The Civil Justice Review set up in 1985 observed that the system was overstretched; the time between the incident that gave rise to the claim and the trial could be up to 3 years for county courts and 5 years for the High Court. Research carried out for Lord Woolf found that the worst delays were in personal injury and medical negligence cases, which took a median time of 54 and 61 months respectively. The average waiting time for a county court claim was 79 weeks. Although time limits were laid down for each stage of the action, both judges and lawyers disregarded them. Often time limits were waived by the lawyers to create an opportunity to negotiate, which was reasonable, but the problem was that there was no effective control of when and why it was done.

According to the 1985 review, long delays placed intolerable psychological and financial burdens on accident victims; they undermined the justice of the trial by making it more difficult to gather evidence, which then became unreliable because witnesses had to remember the events of several years before. The overall result was to lower public esteem of the legal system as a whole.

Injustice

Usually an out-of-court settlement is negotiated before the litigants ever reach the trial stage. For every 9,000 personal injury cases only 300 reach trial. Outside such cases, for every 100,000 writs issued before 1999, fewer than 300 came to trial. There are advantages to reaching such a settlement — a quick end to the dispute and a significant reduction in costs — but it can equally be argued that the high number of such settlements creates injustice because the parties often hold unequal bargaining positions. Finally, the rules on payments into court increase the unfairness of the pre-trial procedures. As Professor Zander observed, the rule is 'highly favourable' to the defendant, and puts pressure on the claimant to accept an offer.

The adversarial process

Many problems result from the adversarial process, which encourages tactical manoeuvring rather than cooperation. It would be far simpler and therefore cheaper for each side to state precisely in the pleadings what it alleges, disclose all the documents it holds, and give the other side copies of its witness statements. Note the almost complete lack of 'judicial trial management'.

Advantages of civil courts

While most students can recite the problems of courts in terms of 'delay, expense and formality', comparatively few can explain the advantages that courts undoubtedly have over any other form of dispute resolution. In a 'comparative' question that asks you to evaluate the respective advantages and disadvantages of different forms of dispute resolution, the ability to explain the advantages will score high marks.

Compulsory process

There is no other process by which you can effectively compel the other side to come to a forum to resolve a dispute. The other party could, of course, decline to lodge a defence or even to appear in court, but, in that case, default judgment would be issued against them.

Formality of procedures

Rules of evidence, disclosure and legal argument all ensure a fair process, supervised by the judge, who is a trained and qualified expert in the law and legal process.

AS Law

Appeal process

No other dispute resolution process allows for appeals. In many tribunals, there is no appellate tribunal and an appeal to the QB Divisional Court is only allowed on a point of law. This is also the position with arbitration. Such appeals are rare.

Legal aid

Although civil legal aid has been greatly reduced in recent years, particularly as a result of reforms in the **Access to Justice Act 1999**, it is still more widely available for court litigation than for any alternative. It is also true that lawyers are more likely to litigate on a conditional fee basis in court than in tribunals, arbitration or mediation.

Law-making and development

Only courts, especially the Court of Appeal and the House of Lords, can, through the doctrine of precedent, make and develop legal rules. Any decision given in arbitration and even in tribunals is in effect a decision for that case alone. It is essential, in the areas of business and taxation, for companies and individuals to know what the relevant legal rules are, and to be able to challenge them through the appellate system to allow the law to develop.

Enforcement of decision

Courts have greater powers to enforce their decisions than any other dispute resolution agency.

The civil justice system after April 1999

On 26 April 1999 new Civil Procedure Rules (CPR) came into force. They constitute the most fundamental reform of the civil justice system in this century, introducing the main recommendations of Lord Woolf. He described the rules as providing 'a new landscape for civil justice for the twenty-first century'.

The reformed rules aim to eliminate unnecessary cost, delay and complexity. The general approach of Lord Woolf is reflected in his statement: 'If "time and money are no object" was the right approach in the past, it certainly is not today.' Thus, the first rule of the CPR sets the overriding objective of the whole system — that the rules should enable the courts to deal with cases 'justly'. This objective prevails over all other rules in case of a conflict. The parties and their lawyers are now expected to assist the judges in achieving this objective.

Dealing with a case 'justly' involves the following factors:
- ensuring the parties are on an equal footing
- saving expense
- ensuring 'proportionality' in the way the case is dealt with in terms of the value of the claim, the importance and complexity of the case and the financial position of each party
- ensuring that it is dealt with expeditiously and fairly
- allotting to it an appropriate share of the court's resources

The emphasis of the new rules is on avoiding litigation by means of pre-trial settlements. Litigation is to be viewed as a last resort; the court has a continuing obligation to encourage and facilitate settlement. As pre-trial procedures are the most important area of the civil process because so few cases actually come to trial, Lord Woolf recommended the development of **pre-action protocols** to lay down a code of conduct for this stage of the proceedings. These aim to encourage:

- more pre-action contact between the parties
- an earlier and more comprehensive exchange of information
- improved pre-action investigation
- a settlement before trial proceedings have commenced

Through establishing a timetable for the exchange of information etc. the parties are better informed as to the merits of their case and so are in a position to settle cases fairly, which reduces the need for litigation. If they cannot settle, the parties should be able to go to trial on a more informed basis and thus ensure that the trial itself can run to a tighter timetable.

Alternative dispute resolution (ADR)

This is greatly encouraged and actively promoted by the court. There is a general statement in the CPR that the court's duty to further the overriding objective by active case management includes both encouraging the parties to use an ADR procedure and facilitating the use of that procedure. An excellent example of the 'pressure' to make ADR successful was provided by the case of *Dunnett* v *Railtrack plc* (2002), where Railtrack, which won the case, was not awarded its costs because it had 'turned down flat' an offer of ADR after the court had suggested that this would be the best way to resolve the dispute between the parties. As the claim by Mrs Dunnett was only for £9,000 and the legal costs of taking the case up to the Court of Appeal were over £100,000, Railtrack made an expensive mistake.

Case management

This is the most significant innovation of the 1999 reforms: the court is the active manager of the litigation. Traditionally, the parties and their lawyers were left to manage their cases; but the new rules aim to bring cases to trial quickly and efficiently, placing the management of cases in the hands of the judges and emphasising the court's duty to take a proactive role in the management of each case.

Once proceedings have commenced, the court's powers of case management are triggered by the filing of a defence and/or counterclaim. The court first needs to allocate the case to one of the three tracks, which will determine the future conduct of the proceedings:

- **small claims** — actions under £5,000
- **fast-track** — actions between £5,000 and £15,000
- **multi-track** — actions over £15,000

Small claims

There is no significant change to previous procedure apart from increased jurisdiction to £5,000. (Its previous jurisdictional limit was £3,000.)

Fast-track

These cases are normally dealt with in the county court. The court gives directions for the management of the case and sets a timetable for the disclosure, the exchange of witness statements, the exchange of expert witnesses and the trial date, or the period within which the trial will take place, which will be no more than 30 weeks later. (Before 1999, trials took place, on average, 80 weeks later.)

In an attempt to keep lawyers' costs down, fixed costs for these trial have been recommended, but the introduction of fixed costs has been delayed until additional information is available. Lord Woolf recommended that there should be a £2,500 limit on costs for fast-track cases.

Multi-track

The court can give directions for the management of a multi-track case and set a timetable for the steps that are to be taken. Alternatively, for more serious cases, the court may fix a case management conference or a pre-trial review or both. The court does not at this stage automatically set a trial date or a period within which the trial will take place.

Criminal courts

The magistrates' court is the 'workhorse of the criminal justice system' and is responsible for hearing over a million cases each year. All summary offences and the majority of 'either-way' offences are tried by magistrates' courts. Within the magistrates' courts are the youth courts, which have the jurisdiction to try all offences charged against those aged from 10 to 17 (excluding murder, which can only be tried in a crown court).

Appeals are made to the divisional court of the Queen's Bench Division of the High Court on a point of law by way of 'case stated', or to the crown court against sentence or conviction.

- **Summary offences** — these can only be tried by magistrates.
- **'Either way' offences** — these can be tried either by magistrates or by a judge and jury at the crown court.
- **Indictable offences** — these are serious offences that are only triable in the crown court.

Crown court

Although the crown court acts as an appeal court, hearing cases from magistrates' courts, the main jurisdiction of crown courts is to hear all indictable offences (such as murder, rape and robbery) and the more serious 'either-way' offences, where jurisdiction has been declined by magistrates or where the defendant has elected to be tried on indictment by a judge sitting with a jury.

Cases are tried by different judges, depending on the seriousness of the offence.

- All Class 1 offences (murder) must be tried by a High Court judge from QB Division. Such judges also try the majority of Class 2 offences — those offences which can result in a life sentence (e.g. rape, robbery, attempted murder).
- Other less serious offences are tried by circuit judges or recorders. In all cases heard in crown courts, the decision on the defendant's guilt or innocence is taken by the jury.

Court of Appeal (Criminal Division)

This is presided over by the Lord Chief Justice (currently Lord Woolf). Three judges make up the panel which hears appeals, usually a Lord Justice of Appeal accompanied by two senior High Court judges from QB Division. In more important appeals, all the judges will be Lords Justices.

Appeals may be made to this court by defendants against sentence or conviction from the crown court, provided 'leave to appeal' has been granted. In appeals against sentence, the Court of Appeal may confirm or reduce the sentence imposed at trial. Additionally, the court may lay down or vary a 'tariff' sentence — this is where the Court of Appeal establishes a clear guideline on sentencing for a particular offence to assist trial judges.

The principal grounds for appealing against conviction are: that the original conviction is 'unsafe or unsatisfactory'; that new evidence which was not available at the time of trial has come to light; that there has been a material irregularity in the course of the trial. The court can uphold the original conviction, quash it (i.e. overturn it and release the defendant), substitute a lower-level conviction (e.g. a manslaughter conviction where the original conviction was for murder) or order a retrial.

Appeals by the Attorney General

The Attorney General, acting on behalf of the Crown Prosecution Service, can, with the leave of the court, appeal to the Court of Appeal against 'an unduly lenient sentence' under s.35 of the **Criminal Justice Act 1988**.

The Attorney General can also refer a case to the Court of Appeal following an acquittal in the crown court which he or she has reason to believe was the result of an error in law made by the judge in his/her directions to the jury. The purpose of such a referral is to verify the correct legal rule. The defendant, having been acquitted, is not identified in the citation, which is simply listed as 'Attorney General's Reference No... of 2002', and, whatever decision on the law is made by the Court of Appeal, the acquittal is not affected in any way.

Criminal Cases Review Commission

This commission was established under the **Criminal Appeal Act 1995** to take over the powers previously exercised by the Home Office to investigate alleged miscarriages of justice, which had been so heavily criticised by the Runciman Royal Commission on Criminal Justice. This independent body, presided over by a lay person, has the responsibility of investigating such allegations. The commission 'must consider that there is a "real possibility" that the conviction, verdict, finding or sentence would not be upheld were the reference to be made'. Examples of such references include the case of Derek Bentley (1998) and the case of Sally Clarke (2003), whose conviction of the murders of her two children was quashed following the disclosure of flawed forensic evidence.

Alternatives to courts

Tribunals

There has been a considerable growth in the potential for disputes between individuals, groups and state agencies. Agencies created for the implementation of state interventionist policies, as in the field of welfare provision, have expanded; this has created in turn the potential for disputes between individuals and social welfare officials, and between property-owners and planning authorities. Frequently, the legislation which has established the machinery for implementing such policies has also set up the institutional framework within which disputes in particular fields are to be resolved, and it is significant that in many such cases the dispute-solving mechanisms adopted have not been ordinary courts of law, but rather specialised **tribunals.**

If all the potential disputes created under the weight of social legislation had to be settled in ordinary courts, there can be no doubt that the court system would collapse under the enormous workload. The courts are, for many of these cases, inappropriate for dealing with such disputes. For example, it would be completely out of place for a county court to have to hear a claim by a social security claimant for a few pounds a week. The usual delays affecting court cases would operate harshly on a claimant needing an immediate decision.

To provide a system for resolving disputes without the trappings of law courts, various governments have introduced, through legislation, a network of administrative tribunals designed to provide *instant* justice cheaply, efficiently and with minimum delay and formality. These tribunals comprise not highly paid judges but panels made up of a chairperson, who is usually legally qualified, and two other, non-legally qualified people, who have expertise in the particular field over which the tribunal has jurisdiction.

Tribunals, which form the largest part of the civil justice system in England and Wales, hear about 1 million cases each year. That number of cases alone makes their work of great importance, since more of us bring a case before a tribunal than go to any other part of the justice system. Their collective impact is immense.

Because tribunals have all been set up by different statutes over a period of time, the problem of diversity between different types of tribunals was one of the key issues addressed by the Franks Committee, which reported in 1957. The result was the **Tribunals and Enquiries Act 1958**, whose provisions are now contained in the **Tribunals and Enquiries Act 1992**. Whilst this diversity has led to a confusing network of tribunals dealing with different areas and incorporating different procedures, it must be remembered that tribunals are *specialised* bodies, dealing with very limited areas, and that this specialisation must be contrasted with courts of law, which have a much wider jurisdiction and hear many kinds of disputes involving different fields of law.

The Franks Committee commented that tribunals should be characterised always by openness, fairness and impartiality. It made various recommendations, most of which were incorporated in the 1958 Act.

- **Openness/fairness** entailed the adoption of clear procedures which allowed parties to know their rights, present their case fully and be aware of the case against them.
- **Impartiality** meant that tribunals should be free of undue influence from any government departments concerned with their subject area. The committee was particularly concerned that tribunals were often on ministry premises, with ministry staff.

The committee recommended the establishment of two permanent Councils on Tribunals, one for England and Wales and one for Scotland, to supervise procedures. Although a council was set up (with a Scottish committee), its functions are only advisory — it has little real power, and cannot reverse or even direct further consideration of individual tribunal decisions.

Advantages of tribunals

Speed

Tribunal cases come to court fairly quickly and many are dealt with in a day. Many tribunals are able to specify the exact date and time when a case will be heard, so minimising time-wasting for the parties. In some tribunals, e.g. employment tribunals, it is common for a process of mediation or conciliation to be used to deal with the case initially. This often results in a solution without the need for a full hearing, which in turn saves further time and expense.

Cost

Tribunals usually do not charge fees, and each party generally pays its own costs, rather than the loser having to pay all. The simpler procedures of tribunals should mean that legal representation is unnecessary and costs will therefore be reduced.

Informality

This varies between different tribunals, but, as a general rule, wigs are not worn, the strict rules of evidence do not apply and attempts are made to create an unintimidating atmosphere. This is obviously important when individuals are representing themselves.

Flexibility

Although tribunals obviously aim to apply fairly consistent principles, they do not operate strict rules of precedent, so are able to respond more flexibly than courts. Very few of their decisions are formally reported.

Specialisation

Tribunal members already have expertise in the relevant subject area and, through sitting on tribunals, are able to build up a depth of knowledge of that area that judges in ordinary courts could not hope to match.

Reduces pressure on courts

Without tribunals all ordinary courts would be completely swamped and delays would be many times worse than they are at present.

Awareness of policy

Because of their expertise, tribunal members are likely to understand the policy behind legislation in their area. They often have wide, discretionary powers which allow them to put policy into practice.

Privacy

Tribunals may, in some circumstances, meet in private, so that individuals are not obliged to have their problems aired in public.

Disadvantages of tribunals

Lack of openness

The fact that some tribunals are held in private can lead to suspicion about the fairness of their decisions.

Unavailability of legal aid

Full civil legal aid is available for only a couple of tribunals — the Prison Disciplinary Tribunal and the Mental Health Tribunal. Although assistance in case preparation is available under the legal help scheme (see pp. 46–49), it will not cover representation. Tribunals are, of course, designed to obviate the need for legal representation, but the fact is that in many of them the ordinary claimant will be facing an opponent with access to the very best representation, e.g. an employer or a government department, and this clearly places him or her at a serious disadvantage. Even though the procedures are generally informal compared to those of courts, the average person is likely to be very much out of his or her depth. Research by Genn and Genn in 1989 found that much of the law with which tribunals were concerned was complex and that their adjudication process was sometimes highly technical. The Free Representation Unit

(FRU) statistics indicated that individuals who were represented had a better chance of winning their cases.

There is some dispute as to the desirability of such representation necessarily involving lawyers. Although in certain cases a lawyer is the most appropriate form of representation, there are fears that the introduction of lawyers could affect the aims of speed and informality. If money for tribunal representation were available, it might be better spent on developing lay representation, such as that offered by specialist agencies, e.g. the UK Immigration Advisory Service or the Child Poverty Action Group, which can develop real expertise in specific areas, as well as general agencies such as the CAB. However, there is no real likelihood of any additional funding being made available by governments.

Involvement of interested parties

The requirement of independence defined by Franks is compromised by the fact that members of some tribunals are appointed by the minister on whose decisions they have to adjudicate. Although there is no evidence that this results in bias, clearly it is difficult for such tribunals to achieve the appearance of impartiality.

Reasons for decisions are not always given

Although the Court of Appeal has strongly recommended that reasons for decisions should be given, and this is a requirement of the **Human Rights Act 1998**, this does not always happen.

Too complex

The 1979 Royal Commission on Legal Services (the Benson Committee) recommended a review of tribunal procedures with a view to simplifying matters so that applicants could represent themselves as far as possible; yet, if anything, tribunal procedures have become more legalistic. The research of Genn and Genn appeared to confirm that self-representation would be very difficult before some tribunals and therefore better legal or lay representation would become even more necessary.

Lack of accessibility

The Franks recommendation that tribunals should be 'open' requires more than just a rule that hearings should usually be held in public; it also demands that citizens should be aware of tribunals and their right to use them. In cases where the dispute is between a citizen and the government, the citizen will usually be notified of procedures to be followed, but in other cases more thought needs to be given to publicising citizens' rights.

Problems with controls over tribunals

Considered together, tribunals vary widely, and make thousands of decisions each year in very different types of case. It is not easy to supervise this diversity. (The Council on Tribunals is a watchdog with no teeth — it is only advisory/consultative.)

Appeals

Sir Andrew Leggatt in his comprehensive report on tribunals stated that:

There is a confusing variety of routes of appeal from tribunal decisions. The system has been rightly described as a hotch-potch. While it is important that there should be effective rights of appeal, in some tribunals there are too many stages, leading to long delays in reaching finality. There should be a right of appeal on a point of law, by permission, on the generic ground that the decision of the tribunal was unlawful:

- from the first-tier tribunals in each Division to its corresponding appellate tribunal
- from appellate tribunals to the Court of Appeal
- where there is no corresponding appellate tribunal, to any such court as may be prescribed by statute

Non-adversarial procedures

There have been recent developments in the UK to encourage the use of non-adversarial procedures in the settlement of disputes, including mediation, conciliation and mini-trials.

The most formal type of alternative dispute resolution (ADR) — arbitration — is described below. ADR schemes have been in use in the USA, Australia, Canada and New Zealand for many years, and have been endorsed by the current Lord Chancellor in the light of major criticisms of the civil justice system and the pressures on legal aid. A court decision offers certainty and finality (subject to rights of appeal), but such decisions are often outweighed by delay, cost and the stress of undertaking litigation.

ADR attempts to involve the client in the process of resolving the dispute. It does not rely on an adversarial approach but rather on reaching an agreement. Each case is decided on its merits without reference to previous cases. The common ground between the parties can be emphasised rather than points of disagreement. It offers a confidential process, and the outcome will not be published without the consent of both parties. Resolution of a dispute can be fast and straightforward, and hearing times and places are at the agreement of both parties.

Arbitration

Arbitration may be defined as the determination of a dispute by an impartial person (rather than a court) after hearing both sides in a judicial manner. It is an increasingly popular way of resolving disputes where both parties voluntarily agree to an independent third party making a decision in their case. It has been described as 'privatised litigation with the judge and venue paid for by the parties'. The process is governed by the **Arbitration Act 1996.**

The arbitrator is usually chosen by the parties and may be a businessman or lawyer or someone with technical knowledge, e.g. an engineer or architect, if that is the basis of the dispute. The date, place and time, the method of arbitration and the powers of the arbitrator are all matters for the parties to decide in consultation with the arbitrator.

There are different types of arbitration:

- **Small claims court**. Although the small claims court takes place as part of the jurisdiction of the county court, in fact the procedure followed is that of arbitration. The district judge is not bound to adopt strict court rules of evidence and procedure, and acts in effect as an arbitrator. The financial limit is £5,000 and most cases involve debt recovery or consumer problems.
- **Consumer arbitration**. The Office of Fair Trading (OFT) has in recent years encouraged and approved many trade association-based arbitration schemes to resolve consumer problems, e.g. the Association of British Travel Agents (ABTA) for holiday problems; similar schemes cover electrical or furniture retailers, dry cleaners etc. Usually, these involve a 'paper' arbitration, where the arbitrator makes the decision after reading the documents of the case, although it may be possible for there to be a hearing where the parties give evidence.
- **Commercial arbitration**. The complexity of business contracts makes disputes likely. One way to limit damage and expense caused by such disputes is for the parties to go to arbitration rather than to the courts. Arbitration is more likely to maintain business relations between the parties than the more adversarial court process. For these reasons many business contracts contain a '*Scott Avery*' clause, whereby disputes must first be referred to arbitration. In such arbitrations, it is likely that the arbitrator will be a member or fellow of the Institute of Arbitrators and as such will have a legal knowledge of the matter in dispute. Note that the Commercial Court (part of the QB Division) can, at the request of both parties, adjourn the court litigation and instead decide the issue by arbitration.

Advantages of arbitration
- Parties retain more control over arbitration than over a court case, where the control is effectively exercised by lawyers and the judge.
- The proceedings are held in private.
- Arbitration is usually quicker and cheaper than court proceedings.
- The arbitrator is not usually a lawyer but a specialist in the field concerned, who has been trained as an arbitrator.

Disadvantages of arbitration
- There is no legal aid.
- Opportunity to appeal is limited.
- There may be difficulty in enforcing awards.
- There may be an imbalance between parties, e.g. consumer against company.

Mediation

In mediation a neutral third party acts as a go-between to facilitate cooperation and agreement. Where the relationship between the parties needs to be preserved, as in family disputes or those involving commercial matters, mediation ensures that the relationship is not soured as it would be by litigation. It is a voluntary process and, should it fail, the parties will have preserved their positions.

The procedure is informal: an independent third party discusses the matter in dispute with each party separately. The mediator is independent and assists the parties in negotiating with each other on disputed points, so that the parties feel in control.

Mediation is widely used in the USA in family and corporate disputes. It can also be used to settle priorities before the start of litigation or, in some cases, in place of litigation. However, its use presupposes a degree of cooperation between the parties, and where parties are entrenched mediation may not be appropriate.

In the UK, commercial mediation is promoted and organised by companies such as International Resolution Europe Ltd and the Centre for Dispute Resolution, founded in 1990 under the auspices of the CBI. Mediation in family disputes is available from the National Association of Family Mediation and Conciliation Services, which offers support to those who wish to conduct their own negotiations and only refers to lawyers in an advisory capacity. Some 300 mediators throughout the UK offer family counselling and legal advice; they are trained solicitors and counsellors, whose aim is to arrive at mutually agreed settlements. Note the importance attached to mediation in the **Family Law Act 1996**, which is aimed at taking divorce settlements out of the courts and establishing family mediation centres throughout the UK.

Conciliation

Conciliation is a 'halfway house' between arbitration on the one hand and mediation on the other, the former being the most formal, the latter the least formal. The conciliator offers a non-binding opinion, which may lead to a settlement. The practice is widely used in the USA to settle commercial disputes. The parties' lawyers present the arguments in the case to the parties and a neutral adviser, who may be a judge or senior lawyer; this enables the parties to assess the strengths, weaknesses and prospects of the case and gives them the opportunity to enter into settlement discussions on a realistic, business-like basis.

Conclusion

The aim of ADR is to facilitate settlement, whereas the aim of litigation is to obtain judgment, but note that, as well as barristers and solicitors, our judges are becoming increasingly involved with ADR. In 1993, a practice statement was issued by the Commercial Court (of the QB Division) to the effect that parties should be encouraged to consider using ADR as an additional means of settling disputes. Judges of the Commercial Court can offer arbitration but not mediation or conciliation — however, the clerk to the court retains a list of bodies offering such services.

The Committee on Alternative Dispute Resolution, established by the Bar Council and chaired by Lord Justice Beldam, published its report in 1991. It approved the notion that the courts should embrace ADR in order to support the judicial process. ADR is widely accepted and potential litigants or their legal representatives follow such processes before resorting to litigation.

In his Access to Justice Inquiry Lord Woolf recommended greater use of ADR, e.g. neutral experts, who assist in reaching a pre-trial settlement; independent mediation; or a separate tribunal or specialist arbitration scheme in small claims involving medical negligence.

Finance of advice and representation

Society requires that all its members keep the law. It therefore follows that all citizens should be not only equally bound by the legal system but also equally served by it. Yet justice, as one judge famously noted, may be open to all, but only 'in the same way as the Ritz Hotel'. In other words, anyone can go there but only if they can afford it. One of the most serious issues that has always confronted our legal system is access to justice — how people can first of all obtain appropriate legal advice and then take a case to court when legal costs are so high.

Since the end of the Second World War, the state has tried to provide a comprehensive system of free or subsidised legal advice and representation. The introduction of such schemes was rightly described by a senior judge as one of the major legal reforms of the twentieth century. However, over the last few years, the bill for these schemes has grown too quickly. Despite government efforts to 'tighten up' means tests, particularly with the Green Form legal advice scheme in 1993, costs continued to outstrip its ability to fund the system. From 1992/93 to 1997/98 spending on civil and family legal aid grew by 35% from £586 million to £793 million, but, at the same time, the number of cases funded actually fell by 31% from 419,861 to 319,432.

These measures led to a situation in which only the very rich, through paying privately, or the very poor, through legal aid, were capable of taking cases to court.

Over the years, lack of funding has led to what is referred to as 'the unmet need for legal services'. Many people find themselves unable to use the services of solicitors and barristers because of the financial limits of legal aid schemes and the high costs that lawyers charge.

You need to be aware of the different schemes which exist to provide legal advice and legal representation, both in criminal and civil matters:
- paying privately for a solicitor

- private legal insurance
- motor or house insurance policies
- 'law for free' work by solicitors (formerly called *pro bono*')
- the Citizens' Advice Bureau
- law centres
- independent advice centres — Age Concern, Shelter
- local authority services — Trading Standards, Environmental Health, housing advice centres, welfare rights units
- Race Equality Councils
- trade union or professional associations
- the Free Representation Unit in London, which handles 1,000 tribunal cases a year on a *pro bono* basis. In 2000, it won awards totalling £500,000. Its role in helping people unable to pay for their own representation increases as legal aid availability is reduced.
- ALAS — the Law Society's free Accident Legal Advice Service, aimed at helping accident victims recover compensation.

In 2000, the Legal Aid Board was replaced by the Legal Services Commission (LSC), which runs two schemes — the civil scheme, responsible for funding civil cases as part of the Community Legal Service, and a separate scheme for criminal cases, the Criminal Defence Service. The LSC has been given significantly more power than its predecessor. It will gain much more control over publicly funded cases through the use of contracts with providers.

The civil scheme

In civil cases, the following schemes are run by the Community Legal Services:
- **Legal help**, which provides initial advice and assistance with any legal problem, but is subject to a tight means test. Help is available from a solicitor or other legal adviser who holds a contract with the LSC. Under this scheme, legal advice up to a limit of £500 may be provided to the client.
- **Help at court**, which allows for a solicitor or legal adviser to speak on your behalf at certain court proceedings without formally acting for you in the whole proceedings, e.g. an application to suspend a warrant for possession in a housing case.
- **Approved family help**, which provides help in relation to a family dispute, including assistance in resolving that dispute through mediation.

Civil legal aid

This funding is controlled by Community Legal Services and deals with all the work involved in bringing an action to court or defending an action in court, including representation. Since the **Access to Justice Act 1999**, all actions for recovery of money damages, especially personal injury cases, have been 'diverted' to conditional fee agreements (CFAs) — see below. Such legal aid funding as is still provided is targeted on child protection cases, cases involving breaches of human rights and 'social welfare' cases, including housing and employment rights.

Eligibility for funding depends on a means test, which considers an applicant's disposable income and capital. Those whose income and capital are below the minimum limits will pay no contributions, but if income or capital is between the lower and upper limits, a contribution must be paid. The grant of legal aid is also contingent on a merits test — that is, the likely success of the case. The funding code stipulates that full representation will be refused unless there is a good chance of success and that the award of damages will exceed the costs of the case.

Conditional fee agreements

Conditional fee agreements (CFAs) were first introduced in 1995 under the **Courts and Legal Services Act 1990** (the implementation of the Act was delayed), which allowed a form of contingency fee. Under this agreement solicitors and barristers can agree to take no fee if they lose and are able, if they win, to raise their fee up to a maximum of double the usual fee. (However, under a voluntary Law Society agreement, this 'uplift' is limited to a maximum of 25% of damages recovered.) The **Access to Justice Act 1999** gave the scheme greater prominence, and the clear intention is that all claims for money damages should be made on the basis of CFAs.

In order to provide against the possibility of losing and consequently having to pay the winner's costs, the Law Society has arranged an 'after the event' insurance scheme whereby, for a relatively small amount, liability for such costs is covered.

Advantages of CFAs
- **No cost to the state**. The costs are entirely borne by the solicitor or the client, depending on the outcome. Supporters of this scheme argue that, as well as saving public money overall, CFAs allow the government to fund properly those cases which still need state funding and to direct more funds towards suppliers of free legal advice, such as the CAB.
- **Anyone can bring a case for damages**. One of the strongest arguments in favour of CFAs is that they allow cases to be brought by many people who would not have been eligible for legal aid or who could not reasonably have been expected to pay contributions under the existing civil legal aid scheme. As long as they can afford to insure against losing and can persuade a solicitor that the case is worth the risk, anyone can bring a case for damages.
- **Raises performance levels of solicitors**. Supporters of CFAs claim that conditional fees encourage solicitors to perform well since they have a financial interest in winning cases funded in this way.
- **Wider coverage**. It looks likely that CFAs may be allowed for defamation actions and cases brought before tribunals — two major gaps in the existing legal aid scheme.
- **Fairness to opponents**. Clients receiving legal aid who lost their cases were not usually obliged to pay the winning side's costs, which was seen as an unfair advantage, particularly where both litigants were ordinary individuals but only one

qualified for legal aid. The insurance requirement of CFAs solves this problem.

- **Discouragement of frivolous or weak cases**. In recent years there have been major problems when apparently trivial cases have been dragged through the courts at public expense, seemingly confirming the view that both solicitors and the Legal Aid Board are unable to apply the merits test sufficiently rigorously. For example, a convicted bank robber received £1,500 by means of a preliminary legal aid certificate in order to bring an action against the police for a new suit to replace the one he was wearing when he was shot by police officers. Solicitors are unlikely to take on such cases, but, if they do, they or their clients bear the costs.

Disadvantages of CFAs

- **Inadequate substitute for legal aid in uncertain cases**. Most of those who have criticised CFAs accept that in uncertain cases they are a good addition to the state-funded legal aid system, but are concerned that CFAs may not be adequate as a substitute for it.
- **Solicitors may only take on cases they are likely to win**. Critics, including the Bar, the Law Society and the Legal Action Group, have expressed strong concerns that certain types of case will lose out under the new proposals. They suggest that solicitors will only want to take on cases under CFAs where there is a high chance of winning.
- **High insurance premiums to cover losing**. Most concern is expressed about medical negligence cases, which are generally difficult for claimants to win — the success rate is around 17% compared to 85% for other personal injury actions. It can often cost between £2,000 and £5,000 simply to carry out the initial investigation necessary to assess whether the case is worth pursuing. In such difficult cases, 'after the event' insurance can be very expensive — in one such case in 1997, the insurance premium was as high as £15,000.
- **Inadequate for difficult cases with low awards of damages**. Another area likely to be hit is that of cases which have enormous public importance but which need a lot of work, are difficult to win, and may attract relatively low levels of damages even if successful, e.g. litigation by cancer sufferers against tobacco companies, or actions against the police or government.
- **Valueless to some litigants**. There are obvious limitations to CFAs in that they would be of no value whatsoever to some litigants. A defendant without a counter-claim cannot pay his lawyer's success fee, nor can claimants seeking a remedy other than money damages, e.g. an injunction for nuisance or a boundary dispute between neighbours.
- **Effect on damages**. Damages are calculated to compensate the litigant for damage done. Originally the cost of both the 'uplift' fee and the insurance premium had to be paid by the claimant; however, in the **Access to Justice Act 1999** the Lord Chancellor allowed such payments to be claimed from the defendant. This change should naturally encourage the defendant to settle out of court; a Court of Appeal case, *Callery* v *Gray* (2002), held that if this happened, the 'uplift' fee should be restricted to only 20%.

- **Possible abuses**. Abuses have already occurred in the USA. Since payment depends on success, unethical practices such as 'ambulance chasing', coaching of witnesses and the withholding of evidence might become all too common features of the legal landscape in the UK, as in the USA.
- **Conflict of interest**. There could be a conflict of interest between solicitor and client. There is already evidence in some cases that lawyers' advice about settlement may be influenced by their need to be paid rather than by the strict merits of any settlement offer. The problem could also be exacerbated by the involvement of insurance companies, which, through the solicitor, could bring pressure to bear on the client to accept an inadequate settlement by threatening to withdraw insurance cover against losing. Finally, there is at least the possibility of solicitors cutting corners to enhance profit, which might lead to allegations of professional negligence.
- **Public uncertainty**. In a research study entitled *Nothing To Lose* (reported in an article by Fiona Bawden, *New Law Journal*, 17 December 1999), the main finding was that clients find CFAs confusing. The researchers concluded:

Only one client understood the operation of the CFA scheme in its entirety. If anyone comes across this client, they should buy him a drink!…The fact is that CFAs are a fantastically complicated way of funding litigation. They are a halfway house hybrid grafted onto the existing litigation system by a government determined to increase access to justice but too squeamish to go the whole hog and introduce US-style contingency fees. The blame for clients' lack of understanding almost certainly lies with the system itself, rather than with high-handed solicitors failing to try to explain what signing up to a CFA involves.

Criminal Defence Service

Unlike legal aid in civil cases, state-funded criminal defence continues to be given on a demand-led basis. This means that, although the total legal aid budget is fixed, there is no set limit for criminal legal aid, and all cases which meet the merits and means tests are funded.

The Lord Chancellor's Department has identified the following problems which have arisen with the provision of state-funded criminal legal aid:
- The cost rose from £507 million in 1992/93 to £733 million in 1997/98 — an increase of 44%. At the same time the number of cases dealt with increased by only 10%.
- Although standard fees are now paid in many cases, the most expensive cases are paid in the traditional way, by calculating the bill after the event. This gives lawyers an incentive to boost their fees by dragging cases out, and these cases take up a disproportionate amount of money.
- The system for means-testing defendants to see whether they should contribute to the costs of their case is a waste of time and money. The test has not stopped some apparently wealthy defendants from receiving free legal aid, and 94% of defendants in the crown court pay no contribution at all.

Under the **Access to Justice Act 1999**, the provision of funding is the responsibility of the Criminal Defence Service (CDS), which controls:

- **the duty solicitor scheme**. This scheme was originally created under the **Police and Criminal Evidence Act (PACE) 1984** to provide a right to legal advice for suspects detained in police stations. It ensures access to a solicitor for advice, and assistance is available 24 hours a day, free of charge and without means or merits tests. At magistrates' courts, there is normally a duty solicitor available to give free advice on a defendant's first appearance if they do not have their own solicitor.
- **the criminal legal advice scheme**. This scheme works in the same way as legal help (referred to on p. 46), with the same strict means test.

Criminal legal aid

This scheme covers all types of criminal proceedings and pays for a solicitor to prepare the case and represent a client in court. It also covers the cost of a barrister, particularly if the case is heard in the crown court. The decision to grant aid depends on the two tests outlined below.

Interests of justice

The court decides whether it is in the interests of justice to grant legal aid. For serious cases, such as murder or rape, it will always be in the interests of justice to provide it. For less serious cases, such as minor motoring offences, the court is unlikely to agree to it. Between these extremes, the court decides on the basis of guidelines set out in the **Legal Aid Act 1988**.

'Interests of justice' criteria include cases:

- where the charge is so serious that, if convicted, the defendant risks the loss of liberty
- where the case involves complex legal issues
- where the defendant is unable to understand the proceedings due to language problems etc.

Financial means

The court looks into the applicant's financial position and the likely cost of the case. Applicants with the lowest means receive free legal aid, whatever the costs of the case. Those with more substantial means will not be granted legal aid if they can afford the likely costs. If the likely costs are large, applicants with reasonable means may be granted legal aid, but the court can require the applicant to pay a contribution towards the cost of the case from both income and capital if he or she appears able to do so. Judges in the crown court are able to order convicted defendants to pay some or all of the cost of their representation. This replaces the current system of universal means testing at the start of the case in the magistrates' courts. If the applicant is cleared of the offence, the court normally refunds all contributions he or she may have made towards legal aid.

As with civil legal aid schemes, the Lord Chancellor's Department has increased the powers of the Criminal Defence Service to control the quality of the services provided at public expense through contracting with private solicitors and by setting up a salaried Criminal Defence Service, which guarantees defendants the right to choose between a private solicitor and a solicitor from the Defence Service. This change has naturally proved controversial. A number of pilot schemes were set up around the country, and a scheme in Scotland indicated that there were no significant savings to be derived from having salaried solicitors employed directly by the CDS.

Criticisms of legal aid

Legal help

Formerly Form 10/Green Form, the legal help scheme was designed to bring in a new range of work, in part to address the issue of the unmet need for legal services for dealing with welfare and similar problems, which individuals have traditionally been reluctant to bring to lawyers. The scheme was largely failing until recently because of the increasing problems of running a profitable solicitors' firm. However, the number of welfare problems dealt with through legal help has started to increase, possibly because of the growing involvement of law centres specialising in this kind of work.

The initial limit for this scheme is thought to be far too low, and, where a barrister's advice or expert reports are required, an extension of legal help will always be needed; applying for extensions can waste time. Public awareness of the legal help scheme and the new areas of need it might be able to help with is generally low.

Legal representation

The major problem is that for most money claims civil legal aid is not available. There is greater emphasis on the use of conditional fee agreements. Where civil legal aid is available, it is still subject to severe means testing, and most people who are eligible are required to make a significant personal contribution. Many claimants have to reject the offer of this state aid because they cannot afford the high monthly contributions demanded.

The statutory charge

This charge is applied to money or property 'recovered or preserved' by the assisted person in any proceedings funded by the Legal Services Commission. The charge may result in the 'claw back' of all the claimant's damages which, as far as the client is concerned, may make the whole action a waste of time. While the charge may be technically just — since privately funded clients also face the risk of losing all their damages to costs — to the legally aided client it does not look like a case of justice being seen to be done.

Recovery of costs

When a legally aided client loses a case, it is difficult, often impossible, for the opponent to get costs back, as would normally happen in a civil case. Clearly, this places the legally aided client at an unfair advantage. There is some provision for payment from the Legal Services Commission, but, although this provision increased after Lord Denning's recommendation in *Hanning* v *Maitland* (1970), being sued by a legally aided opponent is a severe risk for the average litigant. Because of this, justice suffers since costs can be used as a weapon to force an early settlement.

Libel and slander
Assistance for legal representation is not available for such actions, so only the wealthy and powerful can afford to defend their reputations.

Tribunals
No assistance is available for tribunal actions, except in a very few cases.

Criminal legal aid
Research by McConville (1993) suggested that the standards of legally aided criminal defence work are low. Much of it is done by unqualified staff, there is little investigative work and solicitors push clients towards pleading guilty rather than taking time to prepare an effective defence. Since the merits test concentrates on the seriousness of the charge and possible penalty, it is more difficult for defendants to get legal aid for minor offences; sometimes it may be difficult to know whether the merits criteria apply until after a trial has started.

Questions
&
Answers

The Unit 2 examination paper offers five two-part questions of which candidates are required to answer two.

The first part-question is usually a straightforward 'explanation' question which calls for a clear description of the main facts of the topic — this is often in two parts. A common error made by candidates is answering only one part.

The second part-question tends to require more analysis, or it may even be set on another area of law, e.g. part (a) could be on juries, where part (b) is on criminal courts. This means that you must read both parts of the question — there is little point in answering part (a) if you find that you cannot answer part (b).

Each question has a total mark of 30 — this can be split 15/15 or 10/20 or 20/10. You should consider this division when deciding which question to answer. As a general rule, because part (a) questions are largely factual it would be better to choose to answer a question where part (a) requiring explanation is worth 15 or 20 marks.

These mark allocations should also be used as an effective guide as to how much to write. Again, a general rule would be to write at least one A4 side for a 10-mark question (about 350 words), then one and a half sides to answer a 15-mark question (about 550 words) and two full A4 sides for 20 marks (about 700 words). You need to learn the difference in required content between similarly worded questions with differing marks, e.g. a 10-mark question on jury selection would not require any description of jury challenges, whereas for the same question worth 15 or 20 marks you would be expected to include it.

Effective answer planning

Note that the key difference between the A-grade and C-grade answers in this section lies in the fact that the A-grade answers have a very clear structure. This is usually demonstrated by a simple, accurate and relevant opening sentence and by the sequencing of the material. You are strongly encouraged to spend some time at the beginning of the examination planning all your answers.

First, read the question carefully. Are you required to outline, explain, discuss, analyse, compare, evaluate? Next, 'brainstorm' the material that you consider relevant to answer the different issues. Note your ideas down in the form of a 'spider-diagram' or a set of headings and sub-headings. This should help to prioritise the points and to indicate the links between them. An important stage in an ideal plan is to assess how much needs to be written on each component. Finally, ensure that your answer refers to case and/or statutory authorities.

As you study the answers in this section you will see that each A-grade answer contains clear case and/or statutory references. The references are important: the mark schemes usually state an explicit requirement for such authorities — if there are no references, the candidate will not get into the top mark band.

uestion 1

Juries (I)

Describe the selection of juries and their function in criminal trials. (15 marks)

■ ■ ■

A-grade answer

The selection of juries is laid down in the Juries Act 1974, which requires jurors to be aged 18–70 (the Criminal Justice Act 1988 increased age eligibility to 70 from 65), to be on the electoral register and to have been resident in the UK (including Channel Islands and the Isle of Man) for 5 years from the age of 13. Jurors are summoned by random sampling, and then the final 12 jurors are chosen at random for the particular trial by the court clerk.

There are, however, certain people who are either disqualified from, or ineligible for, jury service. Those with a serious criminal record who have served a prison sentence within the previous 10 years or who have had a probation order within the last 5 years are disqualified. Those ineligible include the judiciary and people involved in the administration of justice, the mentally ill and clergy. There are others who, because of their work, may be excused as of right — they include doctors and nurses, and members of the armed forces. A final category is that of excusal at the court's discretion — examples are those with a poor command of English and nursing mothers.

Jurors may be vetted and challenged. Peremptory challenge by the defence (i.e. challenging without cause) was ended by the Criminal Justice Act 1988. Defence may now only challenge a juror with cause. The prosecution may require a juror to 'Stand by for the Crown' but this is rarely employed and it is usual for a reason to be given. More detailed checks on a juror's background may only be carried out with the approval of the Attorney General, and this will be given only in security or terrorist trials.

The function of a jury in a criminal trial in crown courts is to decide the issue of guilt or innocence of the defendant. The jury exercises the role of 'being master of the facts' in the trial, whereas the judge is 'the master of the law.' The jury hears all the evidence in the trial provided by both the prosecution and the defence. Jurors are encouraged to take notes and may ask questions of any witness through the judge. At the end of the trial, after closing speeches by counsel, the judge sums up the evidence and directs the jury on all relevant points of law. In a complicated trial, the judge may provide the jury with a series of questions to assist the jury in its deliberations. The jurors retire to a room where, in strict privacy, they consider their verdict. A foreman is selected to speak for the jury and should lead the jurors in their discussions. If after 2 hours 10 minutes the jurors have not reached a unanimous verdict, the judge may recall them to advise them that a majority verdict upon which at least 10 are agreed will be accepted — this was first provided by the Criminal Justice Act 1967. Only about one fifth of all verdicts are by a majority.

When a verdict has been decided, the jury returns to court and the foreman delivers the verdict to the judge.   *524 words*

> ✐ This answer illustrates well the points made in the introduction to this section of the guide. It deals with both aspects of the part-question — selection and role of juries. It contains a number of statutory and case authorities and has a sound overall structure. As it is a 15-mark question, it is also the required length. (If this had been a 10-mark question, no explanation of jury challenging and vetting would have been necessary.) Note how detailed the description of the role and functions of the jury is. Too often candidates simply write that it is the role of a jury to bring in a verdict of 'guilty' or 'not guilty', without attempting to explain how juries perform their task. Full marks would be awarded.

■ ■ ■

C-grade answer

A jury is a group of unqualified citizens who take part in the English legal system. It will be randomly selected from the electoral register by a computer. To serve on a jury, a person has to be aged from 18 to 70, be on the electoral register and have lived in the UK for at least 5 years from the age of 13.

There are a number of reasons why people may not be able to serve on a jury: if they have committed a serious offence within the previous 10 years; if their jobs are incompatible with jury service, e.g. membership of the armed forces; if their work involves the administration of justice; or if they suffer from a mental illness.

A person may be excused jury service if aged between 65 and 70 years or nursing a child.

Once it has been decided whether a person may sit, he or she arrives at court and will normally sit for a period of 2 weeks. Fifteen names are put into a hat and then 12 are selected to be sworn in as the jury.

The jurors' job is to decide whether the defendant is guilty or not guilty in a crown court trial. They will be directed on legal issues by the judge but they alone will decide the verdict. A jury may now return a majority verdict of 10 to 2.   *236 words*

> ✐ The comparison between this answer and the A-grade answer above is obvious. There are no statutory or case references in the C-grade answer and a particular problem is the 'grouping' of the categories of ineligibility, disqualification and excusal. The main weakness, however, is the very limited explanation of the function of the jury. In the A-grade answer this is described fully. This answer would be awarded 7 or 8 marks.

Juries (II)

Explain and evaluate the advantages and disadvantages of the use of juries in criminal cases. (20 marks)

■ ■ ■

A-grade answer

First of all, it is relevant to note that juries only feature in about 1% of all criminal trials — 97% of all criminal cases are dealt with in magistrates' courts, and of those cases which are set for trial in crown courts about 70% result in guilty pleas. In addition, in a considerable number of cases where the defendant has pleaded not guilty, the jury is directed by the judge to return a formal verdict of 'not guilty'.

However, juries continue to play an important role in our system of criminal justice. Juries allow the ordinary citizen to play a significant part in the administration of justice. This means that verdicts can be viewed as those of society rather than exclusively those of professional lawyers and judges.

It has long been argued that the right to be tried by your peers is a bastion of liberty against the state. This was well demonstrated in *R* v *Ponting*, where a senior civil servant at the Ministry of Defence was charged under the Official Secrets Act with unlawfully passing secret material to a newspaper. He was legally guilty, but the jury acquitted him, believing that his prosecution was politically inspired and no harm had in fact been done to national security. It is also worth noting that dictatorships such as Hitler's in Germany or Stalin's in Russia have never allowed juries.

Trial by jury is over 1,000 years old and this tradition is held in high esteem. This is confirmed by the controversy which arises whenever governments propose to limit jury trial, as is the case at present with the Criminal Justice Bill (CJB).

One of the principal arguments for trial by jury is that of 'layman's equity' — the power that juries, unlike judges or magistrates, have to return a verdict of 'not guilty' even where in strict law it is clear that the defendant is guilty, but in circumstances where the jury considers that a conviction would not be fair. This happened in *R* v *Owen*, where a man who shot and injured the man who had killed his 11-year-old son in a serious traffic accident was acquitted. Other cases demonstrating this are *R* v *Kronlid* and *R* v *Pottle and Randall* (with regard to the George Blake escape).

Juries have been subjected to considerable criticism in recent years in terms of their alleged lack of competence, high acquittal rates (when compared to those of magistrates' courts) and the cost of jury trials. The issue of competence has arisen specifically with reference to complex fraud trials, which can last many months — the *Blue Arrow* case lasted a year. It is argued that the very technical details which are introduced in evidence in such trials cannot be understood by jurors. The Roskill Committee recommended that such cases should be tried by a judge sitting with two qualified assessors, and this recommendation is included in the CJB. However, there

question

are only a handful of such cases a year, and the transfer of these to a single judge with assessors would not materially affect the principle of jury trial.

As regards the high acquittal rate, this is certainly a serious problem in particular areas of England, especially Merseyside. Comparison with conviction rates in magistrates' courts is not helpful since the nature of summary cases is usually much more 'fact-based' and the great majority of defendants plead guilty. One factor leading to higher acquittal rates appears to be the large number of middle-class, professional people who are able to evade jury service through ineligibility or excusal. One of the key proposals in the CJB is the elimination of such categories and this should lead to more representative juries.

The final criticism of cost is not relevant, because the major costs of crown court trials are those of professional judges, lawyers, expert witnesses etc. The average jury cost does not exceed £1,000.

In any considered evaluation, it is hard to escape the conclusion that, while it is clear that improvements can be made to jury trials (and many of these are contained in the present CJB), juries have become an entrenched part of our criminal justice system, and without juries public confidence would diminish. It also remains true that as Lord Devlin once famously stated, 'juries are the lamp that shows that freedom lives'.

719 words

> 🖉 This is a question on a subject which more than any other tends to be answered in simplistic terms, using little more than bullet-points to list 'advantages' and 'disadvantages'. The first paragraph is employed to set juries in a clear perspective, to emphasise the limitations of their role within the English criminal justice system. The essay then develops the key argument in favour of juries — that of 'layman's equity' — and uses case examples as support. The answer goes on to address one of the major arguments against juries — their alleged inability to deal with complex fraud trials. However, far from simply stating this as some form of 'self-evident truth', the assertion is analysed critically. The same treatment is also given to the question of the comparative costs of a jury as opposed to magistrates' courts costs. Finally, as the question requires an evaluation, there is a simple conclusion, introducing one of the more famous judicial quotations. Even though there are omissions, such as 'jury nobbling', this answer would obtain nearly full marks because of the depth of the analysis.

■ ■ ■

C-grade answer

There are many advantages and disadvantages in the use of juries to decide a criminal case. The main advantage is that 12 people making a decision are better than 1. This is because it is more likely to eliminate any bias. Another advantage is that jurors are lay people and are therefore unqualified in law. This means that they should have a more objective view of the case than a lawyer or judge. The jury will also balance out the number of legal professionals.

A great disadvantage of using a jury is that the jurors may not understand everything they hear in court — this can be a particular problem when hearing long and complicated fraud trials. This could mean that they will be unable to make a fair and just decision. A further disadvantage of juries is their cost — crown court trials are much more expensive than trials in magistrates' courts. Another advantage of juries is that they make their decisions in private, which means that they are free from any pressures. This also means that they can make decisions which could be unpopular with governments, as in the *Ponting* case. In such cases, it can be seen that juries can take certain circumstances into account as they do not have to follow the law to the letter.

However, it can also be argued that juries are not entirely free from pressures as 'jury nobbling' occurs in some cases.   *239 words*

📝 This is a typical C-grade answer — the points are mentioned rather than explained or analysed. The issue of juries' ability to try fraud trials is poorly dealt with when compared to the A-grade answer above, as are the other topics of 'layman's equity' and cost. The final issue, that of 'jury nobbling', appears to have been added as an afterthought. 'Nobbling' is not explained and the candidate has omitted to mention that, since the advent of majority verdicts in the Criminal Justice Act 1967, this problem has become far less serious. 10 or 11 marks would be awarded.

Question 3

Magistrates (I)

Outline the jurisdiction of magistrates and consider the advantages and disadvantages of magistrates within the English legal system. (15 marks)

■ ■ ■

A-grade answer

Magistrates play by far the largest role in the criminal justice system as they try about 97% of all criminal trials — all summary offences and most 'either-way' offences. Magistrates also try most offences committed by young offenders (aged 10–17) in the youth court. The only offence which cannot be tried here is murder. Other functions within the criminal justice system include bail applications (under the Bail Act 1976) and applications for legal aid, and the issue of search and arrest warrants.

Magistrates' other responsibilities include the following: the family court — adoption orders and proceedings under the Children Act 1989; the licensing court — for the sale and consumption of alcohol, and for betting and gaming establishments; debt enforcement — council tax, utilities and television licences; sitting with a circuit judge at crown court to hear appeals against sentence or conviction.

Magistrates have historically been an important part of the criminal justice system for more than 1,000 years and they enable members of the community to become involved in the administration of criminal justice. They are the most representative type of judges — unlike our professional judiciary, almost 50% are women with almost 7% drawn from ethnic minorities. They also provide 'local' justice as they have to live within a 15-mile radius of their bench; this gives them a greater awareness of local events and local patterns of crime.

Because they are unpaid, magistrates' courts are the only 'profit-making' component of the criminal justice system as the value of fines exceeds the overall costs of these courts. They are also much quicker in bringing cases to trial than is the case with crown courts, where delays of up to a year are not uncommon.

The most significant disadvantage of magistrates is the serious level of inconsistency in their sentencing. Surveys continue to show that some benches are ten times more likely to impose custodial sentences than neighbouring benches. This is clearly unfair — simple justice demands that similar offenders receive broadly similar sentences.

It is also argued that because magistrates are not legally qualified, this justice is 'amateur justice'. This fails to take into consideration the fact that magistrates are now selected far more carefully and receive much more detailed training than was the case several years ago. The importance of the 'partnership' that magistrates form with a legally qualified clerk needs to be noted. The overall success of magistrates' courts is, however, confirmed by the very low 'success' rate of appeals against both sentence and conviction. *411 words*

This answer does, accurately, what the question requires. First, it provides an outline of the jurisdiction of magistrates' courts, where the emphasis is correctly on the courts' criminal jurisdiction, and summarises their civil law functions. It continues with a more fully argued section on the advantages and disadvantages of magistrates. The key point to note here is that this is not simply a 'list' of each, but a careful consideration of the various issues. There is a vast difference between writing 'magistrates can be criticised because they are not legally qualified' and writing the content of the last paragraph. The answer would score 14 or 15 marks.

Magistrates (II)

Describe how magistrates are appointed. (10 marks)

■ ■ ■

A-grade answer

In order to become a magistrate a person can either apply to the local advisory committee, which exists for every bench, or be nominated by local political parties or voluntary bodies. The statutory qualifications are that the applicant must be under the age of 65 and live within 15 miles of the court within which he or she will normally be working. There is no statutory minimum age, but past and present Lord Chancellors have made it clear that they will not appoint anyone under the age of 27. Successful candidates are required to spend an average of half a day per week on sitting in court. The current procedures for selection and appointment are contained within the Justices of the Peace Act 1979.

Categories of people who are excluded from appointment include police officers, members of the armed forces, undischarged bankrupts and those who have a serious criminal record.

After application or nomination, references are checked, as is the person's criminal record. A shortlist is drawn up by the committee and two interviews are held: the first measures the candidate's general character; the second, which comprises a number of judging and sentencing exercises, assesses the candidate's judgment. After all the candidates have been interviewed, the committee meets to consider the various issues of balance as regards gender. The Lord Chancellor has made it clear that he requires broadly equal numbers of men and women, occupation, ethnic origin and, to a lesser extent, political affiliation and age. The committee will finally recommend names to the Lord Chancellor, who usually accepts these recommendations and will formally appoint the magistrates. At the conclusion of the selection and appointment procedure, successful candidates will be formally sworn in as magistrates at a ceremony conducted by a senior circuit judge.

Before sitting in court, newly appointed magistrates are required to attend a training and mentoring programme. *313 words*

> ⊠ This is well planned and developed. The facts are clearly set out and explained, and there is a sound sequence to the factual material. The qualifications are described first, then the reasons for disqualification, followed by the selection procedures, including the two interviews and the need for a 'balanced bench'. The role of the Lord Chancellor is explained accurately, and the conclusion to this process is neatly presented — the swearing-in of the new magistrates with a brief reference to their training and mentoring programme. This answer would receive the full **10 marks**.

■ ■ ■

C-grade answer

Anyone wishing to become a lay magistrate must be recommended to a local advisory committee. They can be recommended by anyone, including themselves, but more often it is by local trade unions or political parties. The job of the advisory committee is to decide who is suitable for the job and pass on their names to the Lord Chancellor, who can then appoint those people as magistrates in their local commission area.

No formal qualifications in law are required — magistrates are required, however, to live within 15 miles of the court on which they are to sit, and to be under the age of 65 on appointment. Anyone who is a police officer or a traffic warden is disqualified, as are those with a serious criminal record.

Once appointed, they are supposed to sit about 35 times a year.   *139 words*

   This answer is much weaker than the A-grade answer above. There is no reference to statutory authority, nor to the criteria for selection laid down by the Lord Chancellor. Absence of any description of the interviews is a particular weakness. Although quite good on the issue of basic qualifications and those disqualified, this answer comes across as lacking authority. The answer would score just 5 marks.

Question 5

Legal professions (I)

Outline the qualifications and training required to become a barrister and solicitor, and describe the work each profession carries out. (15 marks)

■ ■ ■

A-grade answer

In order to become a solicitor, most people take a university degree, not necessarily in law. If another degree is taken, or a non-qualifying law degree, a further year's study is taken to pass the Graduate Diploma in Law (GDL), formerly the Common Professional Examination (CPE). The next part of the qualifying course is the Legal Practice Course (LPC) which is a 1-year full-time course (or 2 years part-time). Finally, students have to obtain a training contract in a solicitors' firm which lasts 2 years.

After the successful completion of the traineeship, the trainee will be admitted as a solicitor by the Law Society and his or her name will be added to the roll of solicitors. It is also possible for mature entrants to qualify as solicitors by first qualifying as legal executives and then as Fellows of ILEX, after which they take the LPC or the 2-year traineeship. Even after qualification, solicitors are required to attend specialised training courses as part of their Continuing Professional Development.

Entry to the Bar is for graduates only — but it is not essential for the student to have studied law. If the degree is in another subject (or a non-qualifying law degree), the GDL has to be taken. After graduation or completion of the GDL, students have to apply to an Inn of Court and be accepted on the Bar Vocational Course (BVC). If these exams are passed and the required number of dinners have been taken, the student is admitted to the Bar by his or her Inn of Court. Students need to obtain a pupillage in a set of chambers, which lasts 1 more year. This work involves 'shadowing' a barrister, who acts as pupil-master. During this period, students must also follow a programme of continuing professional education organised by the Bar Council. On completion of pupillage, the barrister needs to find a tenancy in a set of chambers in order to practise as an independent barrister.

The work of solicitors is largely non-litigious, although they do have rights of audience in both county and magistrates' courts. Their work involves conveyancing (transferring property rights) and probate (wills and executory work), together with giving general legal advice to clients, which could include family law, employment law or setting up companies etc. Under the Courts and Legal Services Act 1990 (as amended by the Access to Justice Act 1999), solicitors can acquire higher court rights of audience by qualifying as solicitor-advocates — there are at present about 1,000 of these. Most solicitors work within a partnership with other solicitors. Over recent years, in both London and large cities, there has been a trend for law firms to merge to create much larger partnerships, which in turn has led to greater specialisation in the work undertaken by solicitors.

The Bar is a referral profession, i.e. clients have to see a solicitor first (unless they are members of another profession, e.g. accountants, in which case there is direct professional access). Barristers are self-employed and usually work from a set of chambers where they share administrative and secretarial expenses with other barristers. The majority of barristers concentrate on advocacy, representing clients in court, but they also provide specialist advice through counsel's opinions to solicitors. The litigation work of a barrister also includes drafting pleadings prior to the case coming to court. Barristers have rights of audience in all English courts.   *554 words*

🖉 This is a well-balanced answer in which the separate issues of qualification/training and functions of each professional are described fully and clearly. Use of specialised legal language is accurate and there is appropriate statutory reference. The work of solicitors is explained very well — usually, candidates fail to distinguish between the non-litigious work and the court work undertaken by solicitors. The key strength of this essay lies in its balanced plan; its structure addresses all the issues raised in the question. It would receive the full 15 marks.

Question 6

Legal professions (II)

Describe recent changes to the legal profession and comment on the suggestion that it is no longer necessary for there to be two distinct professions of solicitor and barrister.

(15 marks)

■ ■ ■

A-grade answer

During the last 12–15 years there have been many changes to the legal profession: solicitors lost their monopoly over conveyancing in the Administration of Justice Act 1985, but under the Courts and Legal Services Act 1990 they obtained higher court rights of audience as solicitor-advocates and there are now over 1,000 of these. Other changes under CLSA 1990 have seen solicitors become High Court judges, and the growth of large, even multinational firms of solicitors, which has led to increasing specialisation within law firms.

Barristers, too, have seen many changes within their profession — they can now advertise their services, and professional clients can consult directly with barristers. Sets of chambers have merged in recent years, and cities such as Birmingham and Leeds have flourishing sets of barristers' chambers and large firms of solicitors.

These are just a few of the changes that have occurred recently. In the Access to Justice Act 1999, employed barristers acquired rights of audience for the first time, and the Act made it easier for solicitors to obtain higher court rights of audience.

Because of these changes, especially the opportunity for solicitors to advocate in the higher courts and to become senior judges, the question has been raised as to whether it is necessary to have two quite separate branches of the legal profession. Britain is the only developed country in which there are two different professions. In the USA and other European countries, there is only one 'fused' profession, where lawyers specialise in either court or office-based work, but they receive a common training process and are governed by the same professional body.

However, to answer this particular question, it is also essential to consider the very different tasks which each branch — solicitors and barristers — perform. Here, a comparison with the medical profession may be helpful. If one is ill, one goes to see a GP. Only if our GP considers there is something seriously wrong will we be referred to a hospital consultant, who may decide that an operation is necessary. The situation is the same with legal problems. For most of us, the only time we see a solicitor is when we are buying or selling our house, making a will, checking a contract or setting up a company. It is very rare for such 'administrative' tasks to require a referral to a specialist barrister. On such occasions a solicitor asks for a 'second opinion' by way of counsel's opinion.

If a decision is taken by the client to pursue or defend the case in court, the solicitor will instruct a barrister or solicitor-advocate to represent the client in court. In such circumstances, it is necessary also to appreciate that while the barrister may be the courtroom specialist advocate, the solicitor, too, is a specialist — in issuing the proceedings in court to start the action and deal with the pre-action protocols such as discovery and organising witness statements. The process of litigation has to involve both solicitors and barristers. A recent Bar Council survey actually confirmed that for most county court actions (where solicitors already have rights of audience) it is cheaper and more cost-effective for the client to employ a solicitor, who will in turn instruct a barrister, than for the solicitor to carry out all the different tasks of litigation.

Given that most people's legal 'problems' can be and are dealt with successfully by solicitors, and that on the relatively rare occasions where court action is necessary both 'office-based' and 'court-based' lawyers are used, it seems unarguable that the public interest is best served by having two separate sets of lawyers. *599 words*

🖉 This question created many problems for candidates. It illustrates the need for detailed planning as candidates are required first of all to identify various changes that have affected both solicitors and barristers and only then to discuss whether two separate legal professions are needed. The key to answering this question lies in understanding the relationship that exists between solicitors and barristers. Too often students appear to learn only the differences that exist between the two branches without appreciating the way in which they work together. A particular problem is that too many students fail to realise how much legal work is non-contentious (such as conveyancing) or how much litigious work solicitors perform themselves in magistrates' and county courts, and, finally, that even where a barrister is instructed there is still much specialised work to be undertaken by the solicitor. All these individual points are covered well in this answer. The comparison with the medical professions of GP and hospital consultant reinforces the general level of understanding in this answer. It would be awarded the full 15 marks.

■ ■ ■

C-grade answer

Due to two Acts passed within the last 15 years — the Courts and Legal Services Act 1990 and the Access to Justice Act 1999 — it seems true to say that the work of solicitors and barristers has changed so much that it is no longer necessary for there to be two separate professions.

The first of these two Acts allowed solicitors for the first time to have higher-court rights of audience by qualifying as solicitor-advocates. The more recent Access to Justice Act 1999 strengthened this process and solicitors now increasingly advocate in the higher courts such as the High Court and Appeal Courts. Solicitors are now also qualified to become High Court judges and even QCs.

When the two branches of the legal profession were formed in the nineteenth century, they had very different functions — a barrister was to represent clients in court whereas the solicitor would be 'office-based' and if the client's case needed to be litigated in court it was then handed on to a barrister. Now this 'handing over' is no longer necessary.

Thus, it can be argued that there are few differences between the work of each profession except that the Bar remains a 'referral' profession. This means that members of the public cannot go to a barrister directly but must first consult a solicitor. Solicitors can perform more types of legal work than barristers, and so it seems clear that we no longer require two separate legal professions.   *244 words*

> 📝 In comparing this answer to the A-grade answer, you can see how much weaker this C-grade answer is. First, the issue of changes to each profession is only mentioned briefly. Although both relevant statutes are referred to, the conclusions are oversimplified, especially as regards the assertion that 'solicitors now increasingly advocate in the higher courts'. There is no evidence to support this claim — rather the reverse, because few of the 1,000 solicitor-advocates regularly represent clients in higher courts. The historical reference is of very limited value. This answer illustrates a common weakness — the failure to understand the specialised work involved in bringing a case to court, where the work of the barrister and solicitor is interdependent. The solicitor does not simply 'hand over' the case to a barrister. This answer would just qualify as a grade C (8 marks). The absence of statutory references would bring it down to a grade D.

Q7

Judges

Outline the process of judicial selection and appointment and explain the functions of judges in our legal system. (20 marks)

■ ■ ■

A-grade answer

The criteria for judicial appointment were laid down in the Courts and Legal Services Act 1990. They are as follows: district judge — 7 years as solicitor or barrister; recorder — 10 years' rights of audience in county or crown court; circuit judge — same as for recorder; High Court judge — 10 years' rights of audience in High Court or 2 years' service as a circuit judge; Lord Justice of Appeal — same as for High Court judge; Lord of Appeal-in-Ordinary (Law Lord) — 15 years' rights of audience in the High Court or the holding of high judicial office.

The selection and appointment procedure for district judges, recorders and circuit judges is broadly the same. Suitably qualified candidates apply to the Judicial Appointments Department of the Lord Chancellor's Department (LCD) in response to an advertisement. References are taken up, and wider 'secret soundings' are carried out by officials within the LCD. A shortlist is prepared and those candidates are interviewed by a panel of three — a circuit judge, an official from the Judicial Appointment Department and a lay member. The interview panel recommends candidates to the Lord Chancellor, who then makes the appointment.

To become a High Court judge, candidates may either apply in response to an advertisement or be invited by the Lord Chancellor to consider the position. Considerable 'secret soundings' are carried out. In addition, the opinions of all serving High Court judges are sought. Those candidates who are short-listed are then reviewed by the Lord Chancellor and the four Heads of Division (the Lord Chief Justice, the Master of the Rolls, the President of Family Division, and the Vice-Chancellor). Successful candidates are appointed by the Lord Chancellor.

Lords Justices of Appeal are always appointed from the ranks of High Court judges. The Lord Chancellor will invite such judges to consider appointment to the Court of Appeal, having discussed their suitability with existing Lords Justices and Law Lords. The Lord Chancellor then makes a recommendation to the prime minister, who formally recommends the person to the Queen.

Law Lords are drawn mainly from Lords Justices but, since the House of Lords is the supreme UK Court of Appeal, senior Scottish and Northern Irish judges are also appointed. As with Lords Justices, the Lord Chancellor recommends candidates to the prime minister, who then advises the Queen to appoint.

The functions performed by judges depend on the court in which they sit. In civil trials, they preside over the trial, hear all the evidence led by both sides and then make a decision, which has to be presented to the parties in detail. If the judge holds the defendant liable, damages will then be determined. In addition, the High Court

question

has the jurisdiction of conducting judicial reviews, which have grown in number considerably in recent years. This requires judges to assess the legality or reasonableness of decisions or actions of public bodies, especially those of Cabinet ministers.

In a criminal trial in the crown court, the judge has to keep order, decide legal questions such as the admissibility of evidence, direct the jury on the law and sum up the evidence impartially. If the jury finds the defendant guilty, it is then the judge's responsibility to pronounce sentence.

In both the Court of Appeal and the House of Lords, judges have an important 'law-making' role, both through the doctrine of judicial precedent and statutory interpretation. Such senior judges are often asked by the government to hold judicial enquiries following a disaster such as the *Herald of Free Enterprise* sinking or the *Piper Alpha* explosion.   *591 words*

   This answer demonstrates a sound understanding of both parts of the question — the selection/appointment and the role of judges. Note that a question on selection and appointment requires explanation of both the statutory criteria and the selection process itself. The structure of this answer reflects the wording of the question. There is a clear sequence in terms of 'ascending hierarchy' of the judiciary which deals with the selection and role of judges. The answer would be awarded 19 or 20 marks.

Alternatives to the courts

Explain the alternatives to the courts in the resolution of civil disputes. (15 marks)

■ ■ ■

A-grade answer

At present, there are many options which are available in dispute resolution: these include administrative tribunals, arbitration, mediation and conciliation. Considerable impetus has been given to arbitration and mediation under the Civil Procedure Rules (CPR), which gave effect to Lord Woolf's civil justice reforms.

Taking tribunals first of all, these have been established over the last 50 years in particular to deal with many different types of problems — employment, social welfare benefits, immigration, fair rent etc. They have a very limited jurisdiction, unlike courts, and are presided over by a panel comprising a legally qualified chairman and two assessors, who, although not legally qualified, are experienced in the area of the dispute. These tribunals now play the largest part in civil dispute resolution as, between them, they hear over 1 million cases a year. One of the most successful has been the Employment Tribunals which hear over 100,000 cases a year, covering unfair dismissal, discrimination at work and redundancy.

Arbitration has been described as 'privatised litigation' and is the process whereby both parties agree to the appointment of an arbitrator to settle their dispute. This procedure is governed by the Arbitration Act 1996. In many commercial contracts, there is a 'Scott-Avery' clause which effectively compels the parties to resolve any contractual dispute through arbitration. There are three different forms of arbitration: small claims with a limit of £5,000 in the county court; consumer arbitration, using schemes approved by the Office of Fair Trading, involving various trade associations (such as ABTA); and commercial arbitration. This last form can be organised through the Commercial Court (part of Queen's Bench Division) if both parties agree.

Mediation has become much more popular in recent years, having proved its value in America. This process involves a neutral mediator working with both parties to assist the parties themselves to reach an agreed solution. No decision is imposed and the parties retain the right to litigate if mediation fails. It is said that while court-based litigation, and to a certain extent arbitration too, is 'rights-based', mediation allows the parties' individual interests to be better represented.

Conciliation can be described as a kind of 'halfway' house between mediation and arbitration. Here, the conciliator, a neutral third party, after discussing the problem between the parties, offers a non-binding opinion to try to resolve the dispute.

385 words

     e This is a strong answer to the question. It has an effective introduction, followed by a full description of each type of dispute resolution with good illustrative examples. The answer contains clear legal references, and the candidate has described each separate procedure clearly and accurately throughout. As this essay is a little short for a 15-mark question, it would receive 13 or 14 marks.

■ ■ ■

C-grade answer

There are various ways of resolving a dispute other than through the civil courts.

- Negotiation — this is where the parties discuss the issues of the dispute with each other, either verbally or in writing, in an attempt to resolve their dispute. Usually, the lawyers for both sides carry out this negotiation.
- Mediation — this is where the parties are joined by a mediator, who is an unbiased and neutral third party. He or she listens to both sides and guides them towards an agreed settlement.
- Conciliation — here the two parties are again joined by a neutral third party who will, at the end of the process, provide a non-binding opinion as to how the parties should resolve their dispute by reaching a compromise agreement.
- Arbitration — this is where the two parties allow a neutral person to decide the outcome. The arbitrator, who is qualified to resolve the dispute, is appointed by the parties themselves. The parties agree to be bound by the arbitrator's decision. Many consumer problems are resolved using this procedure in the small claims court or through trade bodies.

179 words

The contrast with the A-grade answer is stark — this answer is weaker in every sense. There is no statutory authority, and the explanations are very limited. The failure to refer to tribunals is quite a common one, and inevitably results in loss of marks. In terms of style, too, the answer is poor — this bullet-point answer style should be avoided unless there is a severe time problem, or a justifiable reason for using a listing technique, as in the A-grade answer to Question 9. This technique almost always results in an unconvincing answer, unless there is additional factual explanation. This answer would just manage to obtain a grade C (7 or 8 marks).

Access to justice

Explain how someone who wishes to bring a civil action against another person may obtain and finance legal advice and representation. (20 marks)

■ ■ ■

A-grade answer

There are many ways in which legal advice in a civil action may be obtained.

- A private solicitor can be consulted and, if considered necessary, counsel's opinion could also be sought from a barrister.
- Subject to a strict means test, legal help — a form of state-financed legal aid from the Community Legal Service (CLS) — can be obtained, which will provide legal advice from a solicitor or other person who has a contract with the CLS to provide such assistance, up to a limit of £500.
- The Law Society ALAS scheme (Accident Legal Assistance Service) can help accident victims to gain compensation.
- Citizens' Advice Bureaux or law centres both offer free legal advice: law centres employ both solicitors and barristers and their most common types of work involve housing, planning, employment, welfare and consumer problems.
- Private legal insurance or legal cover in a car insurance policy can be used in the case of a car accident.
- Trade unions or professional associations usually have a legal department which will provide advice to members.
- A conditional fee agreement (CFA) can be made, under which a solicitor agrees to take the case on a 'no win, no fee' basis: the CFA was introduced in the Courts and Legal Services Act 1990 and was extended to all money claims in the Access to Justice Act 1999.
- Claims firms have begun to advertise their services widely and operate a form of conditional fee scheme.

> ✍ The first point to note is that this question as usual is in two parts — the first relates to the issue of obtaining legal advice, the second with representation in court proceedings. These are quite separate processes. Although bullet-point writing is rarely to be recommended for essay answers, there are occasions when it can be used to good effect. Here, where there are a number of different ways to obtain legal help, such a list, accompanied by little explanation, enables the candidate to deal with the first part of the question quickly and effectively.

If, after receiving legal advice, the client decides to take the case to court, again there are several ways in which such a case could be financed. The client could instruct a privately paid solicitor to issue proceedings or to defend the case, and then to brief counsel to represent the client in court. Civil legal aid availability has been significantly reduced following the extension of CFAs to all money claims as a result of the

Access to Justice Act 1999. However, it is available — subject to means and merits tests — in cases concerning child welfare and in social welfare cases including housing and welfare benefit actions. In such cases, funding will pay for the solicitor to prepare the case and for the barrister who will represent the client in court.

If the client is pursuing a money claim, seeking compensation from a defendant, the most likely source of financing the case will normally be through a CFA with a solicitor. The solicitor draws up the agreement to carry out the work on a 'No win, no fee' basis, but subject to the requirement that, if successful, he will be able to obtain an 'uplift fee' of up to 100% of his usual fee, provided that this does not exceed 25% of the award of damages under a Law Society agreement. To ensure that an unsuccessful client does not incur liability for paying the winning side's costs, this scheme requires the client to take out an insurance policy which will pay such costs. Under the Access to Justice Act 1999, the costs of this insurance policy and the uplift fee element can be claimed from the other side if the case is won. In the case of *Callery* v *Gray* (2002), the Court of Appeal held that both the success or uplift fee and the policy cost could be reclaimed from the other side even where the case had been settled before the court action commenced, but in such cases the uplift fee should not exceed 20%.

Other schemes which can assist litigants financially are the Free Representation Unit, whereby barristers will represent clients in courts or tribunals on a *pro bono* basis, now called 'Law for Free'. It is also possible for the client to act as a litigant in person (LIP), to represent himself in court, and this is becoming more common. Finally, it may be possible to use the services of a 'McKenzie friend', a person who, although not legally qualified, is able to assist a client in court by providing guidance through the legal procedures and asking witnesses questions etc.   *676 words*

> ✒ The second part of this answer, where more detailed explanation is required, follows a more conventional essay-writing style. In the light of recent changes in legal aid provision, which are clearly explained, the preferred approach here is to concentrate on representation through conditional fee agreements, which form the main focus of this answer. The essay would receive full marks.